How to Change Your

TIME
FOR A
CHANGE

The Re-Entry & Re-Career Workbook

KENT BANNING • ARDELLE FRIDAY

Printed on recyclable paper

VGM Career Horizons
a division of *NTC Publishing Group*
Lincolnwood, Illinois USA

Library of Congress Cataloging-in-Publication Data

Banning, Kent B.
    Time for a change / Kent B. Banning, Ardelle Freiheit Friday.
        p.   cm.
    Includes bibliographical references.
    ISBN 0-8442-4396-5
    1. Career changes.   I. Friday, Ardelle F.   II. Title.
HF5384.B355 1995
650. 14—dc20   95-2573
                                                                CIP

Published by VGM Career Horizons, a division of NTC Publishing Group
4255 West Touhy Avenue
Lincolnwood (Chicago), Illinois 60646-1975, U.S.A.

5 6 7 8 9 0 VP 9 8 7 6 5 4 3 2 1

Contents

About the
Authors

Kent B. Banning is a writer and job search consultant and former director of education for the Arizona Multihousing Association where he administered management programs and taught courses in personnel and business.

Banning graduated from the University of Connecticut with a major in industrial psychology and a minor in business administration and completed the U.S. Air Force Career Guidance School in Denver. He was assigned as a career guidance specialist to counsel, retrain, and reclassify military personnel with obsolete job skills; to conduct skill evaluations; and to convene classification boards for military personnel.

For more than twenty years, Banning was a member of the staff of the University of Connecticut as business advisor and department head, providing administrative services for up to sixty private-sector associations affiliated with the university. He served on search committees to evaluate professional-level personnel and was the OEO/affirmative action representative for private- and public-sector employees. He served as lecturer in purchasing, personnel administration, and business for the adult continuing education center.

In 1979 he became business manager of a private school in Scottsdale, Arizona; in 1982 he contracted to write a book on small business management and spent the next two years as a writer and counselor in job search and résumé preparation, work he continues in today.

Ardelle Freiheit Friday is a medical social worker who began her career as a registered nurse.

After leaving the world of paid employment for several years while she raised her family, Friday took a refresher course in nursing and learned that returning to her former profession would require starting at "ground zero." Instead, she made the decision to apply her accumulated education credits and life experiences toward a new career, which was to be in social work and sociology.

During her years as a returned student (they called themselves "retreads"), Friday had contact with many people who were doing the same as she. It was from these associations that she first became aware of and interested in the career change process. There were no recognized support systems for the returning student. In an informal way, the "retreads" became their own support group, in which Friday participated.

After completing her degree, Friday sucessfully reentered the work force and became employed as a medical social worker in the health care industry. She continues to counsel persons in career transitions, many of whom are adapting to critical changes in their life-styles due to temporarily or permanently changed physical abilities and aptitudes.

Preface

Whatever your reason for pulling this book from the shelf and deciding to invest your time in reading it, we hope you will find something in it to which you can relate. That is the kind of book we want this to be, because it was written with the help of many persons who shared their own experiences with us. We have included their stories throughout the book.

The methods we have suggested using to accomplish an organized process of career change are fairly basic—not too difficult to follow. They have developed in part as a result of twenty years of observing and listening to people in transition. Many of those people were willing to offer their advice for others who would be following the same path toward career change and reentry into the work force. Their hindsight aided the development of our suggestions. This book does not come from a purely academic approach either—both authors have been through the career change process.

Our personal interest in the process of changing careers grew from our own experiences. The more contacts we had with persons in these phases of transition, the more real the problems they encountered became. We began holding formal interviews with men and women ranging in age from their early twenties to mid-sixties. Some were married, others were divorced. They came from various segments of society. Some had no education beyond the high school level while others held advanced and graduate degrees. We interviewed persons who were in one phase or another of the process and still others who had completed the change. Several had more than one career change. Most knew of others who had gone through this experience and felt that their story too was worthy of our hearing. We had no shortage of willing subjects.

Beyond the individual and composite stories we have cited as examples throughout the book were many, many others which together appeared to form a number of patterns. Gender was one of the most obvious trends. For instance, we found that reentry, for the most part, was a female experience. The exceptions were cases where males had been out of the work force due to long or disabling illnesses. Generally reentry was a problem of women who had interrupted educations, first jobs, or career efforts to remain at home during child-rearing years. Some had remained out of the work force longer than others. For all people making a reentry, the length of time out of the work force had a bearing on their skill levels and their self-confidence. The longer they were out, the more they had lost of both and the more difficult it was for them to find a suitable reentry position.

When we first started looking at the problems specific to reentry, we thought of it as a separate transition. We soon discovered that reentry correlated significantly to career change. With rare exception, those persons preparing to reenter the work force also were feeling it necessary or advantageous to change careers at the same time. Their reasons fell into similar groupings. Some, especially women who had left jobs at an early age, had not developed or advanced their former careers to any degree. They were seeking more challenging, better-paying positions than those they had left. Those who had been away from their first careers for a long time felt returning to the same field would mean starting at the bottom again. This was also true of those whose careers involved technical skills. Many were hoping that making a change would be a way to make up for lost time in another area that would offer quicker advancements. Some had developed new interests and skills through life experiences; others were prepared to get additional education to fulfill a dream they had previously set aside.

Age was probably the other most significant trend in the pattern. We divided the interview data into four age groups: from twenty to thirty, thirty to forty, forty to fifty, and fifty to sixty. While there were exceptions, each group appeared to hold a great deal in common in both the reasons they sought a career change and the problems which beset them in transition.

With the group from twenty to thirty years of age, it appeared that career changes were most often contemplated for financial gain and were voluntary. Many changes evolved from "horizontal jockeying." Some did this within one place of employment, but more were moving from one job to another. Future gains in potential promotions, development, challenges, and finances were major considerations. Career changes in this age group frequently appeared to directly influence a change in life-style as well. Sometimes relocation contributed to this change. Young children were often involved, and their welfare presented limitations and numerous concerns. Other limiting factors were time and money. Few had enough of either to use in lengthy preparations for their career changes.

For people in the thirty to forty age group, there were some other considerations. Financial gain was still a goal and often a catalyst, but job satisfaction also rated high. Many of these people had invested ten or more years in their first career. They had finally come to the realization that that career was not taking them where they wanted to go, or they realized that they had chosen a career that really did not suit them. These were the persons who made voluntary changes. The number of women who were voluntarily preparing for reentry increased as their children reached the age of comparative independence. There were others in this age group who were being forced to change due to industrial dislocations or career obsolescence. Relocation was complicated by families. There was also a tendency for members of this group to make career changes from their present industry to a related field, apparently in an attempt to salvage as much knowledge and experience as possible.

With the forty to fifty-year-old group, there was an increase in the involuntary, forced career change. There was a high incidence of divorce as the initiating factor. Following a divorce, many women found it necessary to return to the work force to support themselves and their children. Men found that divorce meant increased financial needs, and some used the career change to reestablish or rebuild their lives. Relocation was sometimes coupled with these changes for both men and women. For the most part, these people had a high level of transferable skills, particularly at the managerial and professional levels. This was also a period in their lives when they had an effective networking system going for them. Most had high expectations of making lateral changes with the same or better salary levels. Some were successful in this, and some were not. As a whole, this group showed creativity and determination, which was a reflection of its confidence level. From the standpoint of the balance of skills and experience, this was perhaps the best time to make changes.

In the final group, people between the ages of fifty and sixty, the predominent obstacle was age. Females and males alike were affected. Confidence levels remained high for those in their early fifties but diminished as age increased. Many found that their salary expectations for a new career were becoming unrealistic. Security took on even greater importance. The involuntary need to make a career change outweighed the voluntary choices to do so. We found a growing awareness and concern for the effect that age had on influencing the market and the availability of options. This was often met with considerable, but understandable, bitterness. Many were frustrated with potential employers who ignored or downgraded their past accomplishments.

Basic to the premise for this book was our belief that more and more career changes are being made. Our greatest concern stemmed from the problems we witnessed people having in making the decisions necessary for change and in successfully completing the transition from former career to new. As we observed, listened, and later put our data in order, one of the crucial factors seemed to be the approach these individuals used in making their changes. Some had gone about it in an organized and orderly fashion while others seemed to struggle on endlessly, suffering one setback after another. One of our interview questions was what advice these people had to offer someone else in their situation. Overwhelmingly their answer was to "have a plan," "be organized." This answer came from those who had lived by this advice as well as from those who had muddled through the experience one way or another.

Our collected data clearly indicated that those who were able to take time to form and follow a plan were much better able to get through the process with less evidence of stress. Those who were dealing with a personal crisis in their lives especially benefited from taking time out in order to do some clear thinking and plan ahead. Not all who were faced with a crisis situation were fortunate enough to have the luxury of doing nothing—not working until they could formulate and carry out a plan. Many did need to take a job, any job, in order to provide for their immediate financial needs. However, the planners accepted these jobs as a temporary stopgap measure until they could proceed step by step with their plan toward something better. Those persons who merely reacted to their crisis circumstances—who had not worked out a long-range plan—also accepted what they felt were temporary jobs, but they tended to stay on in them longer, even when they were unhappy doing so. Without an overall plan, some of these same persons made another hasty decision about their career change—often simply because another opportunity presented itself—and again they found themselves less than satisfied by the change. We found several who had made a succession of starts only to be disappointed each time. During our interviews, it was apparent that they were still unsure exactly what they were looking for. On the other end of the spectrum, we found that the planners seemed enthusiastic and positive about their lives, even though they might be doing double duty by working and carrying out their preparations for a new career.

The emotional states of individuals at the beginning of their career change process also showed patterns. Almost all showed elements of fear, anxiety, anger, and lack of self-confidence—even those whose change was a happy, well-planned event. How they worked through these emotions had a direct bearing on the rate of their progress and the success of their outcome. That is the reason we felt, in this book, it was beneficial to begin the process of change with a discussion of the emotional aspects.

Each of us wants to think of ourselves as being stable and mentally well. For the most part and most times in our lives, we are. But when we must deal with major change in our lives, it can be scary and make us feel very off balance. Sometimes emotions gain the upper hand and rule our thinking process. We found emotions creating blocks for many of our contacts. It appeared that those who never worked through their anger, for instance, remained angry individuals as they sought new careers and employment. Once through the transition of change, they found new sources with which to identify old feelings, such as new associates who they claimed were not open and accepting of them. The adjustment to their new career was made more difficult by their own perceptions and attitudes. What they seemed to fail to recognize was that, though they were directing their work efforts toward something new, they brought their old selves to do the job. They had not rid themselves of the emotional "garbage" that brought them to the need for change in the first place. Those persons who had recognized the effects of their emotional states were the ones most likely to want to work on improving them. These individuals appeared to be aware of the need for planning and were also the most likely to seek assistance in formulating and carrying out their plans.

Some other observations had to do with the type and level of occupation the individual had. For example, those persons with semiskilled and skilled trades appeared to have the most transferable skills. The drawback here was that these persons usually had to accept starting at a lower skill level in the new trade of their choice, particularly those involved in unionized employment.

Professional careers, those requiring academic credentials, often had a similar pecking order. Academic knowledge alone was not a guarantee of placement in a new career, as most employers were inclined to expect and reward experience as well. Those making a reentry into a profession often found it necessary to take refresher courses in order to be recertified. This was especially true of those in licensed professions.

The management and the sales and marketing people were sometimes the most unrealistic in their expectations. Many felt that if they managed one type of activity, they could manage anything. Most employers, however, seem to be more comfortable hiring managers with previous experience in their specialized area. The same is generally true of sales. Drastic changes in the type of product or service being sold require adjustments in attitude, philosophy, and methods as well as additional knowledge. Therefore, the transition in these cases does not usually end with merely the accomplishment of gaining new employment.

Perhaps one of the most difficult persons to place in a new career is the person whose experience is limited to one job. We found this in the forty-plus age group, particularly in those who had taken or been given early retirements (military, government employees, and industry where early retirement is offered in lieu of cutbacks). This is not to imply that those persons may not have considerable transferable skills, but in some situations we encountered, it was a problem. Unless the mail carrier, pilot, X-ray technician, farmer, teacher, minister, and so on had broadened their skills or developed other interests, they needed to be very creative in order to find a second career that would be very different from the first.

A last comment for those of you who are contemplating continuing your education: the very thought of returning to school can be anxiety producing. It evokes a lot of self-examination and self-doubt as to whether you can compete with current, usually young, students. We found without exception that fear was ill-founded. Life experience is the equalizer. Returned students found that they could compete on the same level as their previous academic achievements or higher.

We are indebted to those who have shared their experience with us and are hopeful for those who follow in their footsteps.

Introduction

High technology, foreign competition, permanent relocation, the computer revolution, robotronics, technical obsolescence, the sunbelt, industries-on-the-move, the mobile generation— all are terms you see in the headlines every day. These terms describe the forces that continue to create profound changes in how, why, and where Americans work and why they change jobs. The past four decades have seen dramatic changes in how people work. Many of our current jobs were not even imagined forty years ago, and many jobs that existed then have simply disappeared.

During the first half of this century, most Americans worked in the same community and at the same type of job all their lives. Often they worked at the same occupation as their parents. The job was a means to earn a living, to put food on the table, and to put a roof overhead. The concept of the job being part of an orderly plan of progression, that is, part of a career, was reserved for highly educated members of a profession.

Most jobs required little or no formal education or training. Workers learned on the job. Advancement was a matter of how well that particular job was learned. The longer a person worked at a job, the more difficult it was to change to a different one. Except for those involved in a profession or in management, the job was not expected to provide any real personal satisfaction.

Although the Depression had some impact on the types of jobs available, the beginning of the major changes took place because of World War II. The development of war industries and the shrinking of industries not related to the war effort resulted in considerable employee relocation. Men and women entering the service became accustomed to moving from one part of the country to the other and became involved in learning new skills far removed from their previous jobs. As a result, the old concepts about a job began to break down. Developing technologies required specialized training and knowledge. The G.I. Bill provided the means to meet the demand for specialists by paying for veterans' training and education. Most important, the opportunity to seek a career instead of a job was now open to a significantly larger part of the American work force.

One of the basic differences between a career and a job lies in the amount of time and money spent in preparation. Two to four years in a technical school or a college—six to ten years for those entering the professions—represented tremendous investment. Those spending the time and money expected to remain in that career the rest of their lives. Most major corporations had the same expectations as they structured career paths within the company.

Even so-called entry-level jobs, those requiring little training, began to develop long-term implications as skill levels and job progressions became part of the internal structure of the company or organization. "Job security" and "seniority" became the rallying cry of the labor unions. Government entities developed elaborate career progressions and pension enticements to encourage long-term commitments from employees. Throughout the late forties and the fifties, the concept of a lifetime career or job became firmly established as part of the American dream.

Oddly enough, the very forces that gave birth to the concept of a lifetime career now began to endanger that concept. Entire industries began to relocate, some industries went into rapid decline, foreign competition became a serious threat, and the tempo of change began to accelerate in scientific, high technology, and industrial enterprises.

The sixties became the era of change. Advances in electronics and computer technology had a dramatic effect upon the basic structure of almost every industry in the United States. The era of massive change had begun, and the concept of a lifetime career for everyone began to lose its validity.

The seventies continued the forces affecting the job market in the sixties. Foreign competition continued to increase. A worldwide energy crisis disrupted the labor market as the world economy adjusted to soaring petroleum costs. Specific types of jobs emerged and then disappeared within a decade. Jobs within the high-tech industries were in a constant state of change, requiring employees to continuously update their skills or leave. Under these conditions, it is no wonder that changing careers two, three, or four times within a lifetime has become the pattern for a significant part of the population.

In the eighties and now, in the nineties, career changing has become a part of the work ethic. Changing careers is no longer viewed as an admission of failure, because most employers now recognize the changing nature of the workplace.

Another major transition has been taking place within the work force. Dramatic increases in the percentage of working women have changed the composition of the labor market. Many of these women are returning to the job market after years of voluntary unemployment—raising families, caring for parents, and so on—and therefore are planning new careers.

In general, those involved in the job search process can now be grouped into three broad categories:

1. those searching for positions within an occupational area in which they have had education, experience, and training, the so-called normal career path progression

2. those reentering because their career path was interrupted by extended periods of voluntary unemployment—marriage, raising a family, illness, or other personal reasons

3. those who had established career patterns and, for voluntary or involuntary reasons, now wish to change career direction.

Planning a second or third career is a far more complicated process than searching for a position within a career that is already well directed. Our objective is to concentrate on the elements of the job search that are unique to those changing careers or reentering the work force and to offer guidelines for a successful adjustment to change and identification of a new career direction.

Planning A Second Career 1

It would seem logical to assume that planning a second career would be much simpler than beginning the first one. After all, you are more mature, more knowledgeable about many of the careers available, and more experienced in interpersonal negotiations. Chances are that you have already had direct contact with several types of jobs. Therefore, deciding upon another career should be a breeze—no problem at all.

Unfortunately, those factors, such as maturity and experience, that would seem to make second career planning so simple actually complicate the process. One of the most significant changes that has taken place in your life is that you have lost much of your naiveté. You have a much different picture of the world of work than you did when you went out to look for your first job. And the reason for that different perspective is twofold: you have changed, and the world of work has changed. Planning your second career must take these changes into consideration.

Before any progress can be made in second career planning, two very important questions must be answered. First, do you desire to change your career direction after being continuously employed, or do you desire to reenter the work force after a significant period of being unemployed? The second question to be answered is what are the precise reasons you are considering a second career? The answer to the first question—career change or reentry—will determine the type of evaluation of previous experience and training most appropriate to your situation. The answer to the second question—the reason for planning the second career—will determine how much and what type of mental or emotional preparation will be necessary before you are ready to even start the planning process. The majority of cases involving career changes or reentry are involuntary. That is, most people are forced to change their career direction or reenter the job market for reasons completely beyond their control. These reasons can be personal or job related or, in some cases, a combination of both. It is necessary, then, to carefully examine both the type of planning and the reasons for the planning before an effective job-search program can be developed.

Reentry

Reentry into the job market is predominantly a women's issue, although certainly there are circumstances such as illness or job obsolescense that place men in the position of rentering after prolonged periods of unemployment.

Most women reenter the job market for three reasons. Each of these reasons, however, involves an entirely different set of pressures, anxieties, and fears. Those who reenter the job market voluntarily have the least emotional stress and the greatest opportunity for a logical and unpressured approach to the job search.

The need for new challenges

Women in this category are in the most enviable position. The decision to reenter the job market is purely voluntary and unhurried. There is no financial pressure to find a position immediately. Usually there is sufficient time to seek a career direction, and, if necessary, there is also time to obtain the desired training or education to pursue that career. There is usually a family, relative, or friendship support group, although in some cases there may be some resistance from the family. The reasons for the resistance may be varied. In some instances, a husband may read his wife's desire to find a job as a threat to his role as the sole breadwinner and his conception of the traditional roles of husband and wife. In other instances, the husband or the children or both will resent the fact that the job will take away time formerly spent taking care of their needs.

If you fall into this category—looking for new outlets and challenges—you must give full consideration to your motives. If you are searching for something challenging, something that will offer you a sense of direction rather than something temporary that will provide you with a little extra spending money, just a job is not the answer for you. Usually someone in your position should be looking for a career, not just a job, because your needs are more than monetary. You should look for a position that will offer long-term opportunities for growth and involvement.

If the decision to return to work is a spur-of-the-moment decision, a move brought about because you are bored, then take the time to think about the actions that you are about to take. In all probability there are some long-term implications for your actions.

- As noted before, you will probably continue to work for an extended period of time. Why trade boring housework for a boring job?

- You are probably thinking about reentry in order to satisfy your ego needs—self-respect, a sense of accomplishment, a means of reestablishing self-worth, a new sense of direction—even though you may not have recognized the extent of these needs.

- Although at this point financial need is not your reason for reentry, there is no guarantee that this need might not exist in the future. Circumstances do change, and all you have to do is look around to see how many of your acquaintances have been affected by divorce, death, or business reverses. These or other types of unexpected events have drastically changed their lives and their needs.

The most valuable thing that you have is time—time to think, time to evaluate your previous schooling and experience, and most important, time to finish or supplement your education or training. You are not limited to those jobs that are available to you based on your current educational and training levels because you have the time to develop and obtain a long-term career goal.

Worksheet: Career Planning for Voluntary Reentry

1. List your reasons for reentering the job market.

_____

_____

_____

2. What is an acceptable time frame for reentry for you?

_____

_____

3. List below the careers that interest you.

_____

_____

_____

_____

_____

4. What skills have you learned in previous employment that could be applied to your choices?

_____

_____

_____

_____

_____

5. Do you need to attend an educational institution or trade school for new credentials? Can you afford this, in terms of both time and money?

_____

_____

_____

6. Are you looking for a challenging position? If so, list below the type of challenges that you will find stimulating.

_____

_____

_____

_____

_____

7. List the career fields that meet both your needs and time frame.

_____

_____

_____

_____

_____

_____

_____

***Personal or family
financial needs***

It is no secret that many American families have found it difficult, if not impossible, to exist on one income. For most, the only logical source of a supplemental income is the wife. Consequently the number of working wives has more than doubled over the last decade. Perhaps the most significant factor in the economy causing this increase is the cost of single family homes. In 1988, the median cost of a single family home was in excess of $100,000, thus eliminating many families from the housing market because they did not earn enough to qualify for a mortgage. During the period from the late seventies to the present, many have been able to buy only because the wife's income was included as household income. Therefore, the total of the wife's and the husband's income was sufficient to qualify.

Qualifying to buy a house is only one of the financial reasons that wives have returned to the work force. Just a few of these other reasons include the following:

- The husband has been laid off for a significant period of time.

- The husband's income is not sufficient to afford an acceptable standard of living.

- The husband's income may be enough for the essentials but not enough for such things as recreation, a second car, or some desired luxuries.

- Additional income is necessary for the children's educational costs.

Again, identifying the reasons for wanting to return to work is essential to the job search process. The major difference between the various reasons for returning to the work force listed here is time—the length of time that you anticipate remaining in the work force to accomplish what you want to accomplish. For example, in a layoff situation, the time may be measured in weeks or months. Paying for the children's education may be measured in a few years. Qualifying to pay a mortgage may mean the rest of your employable life. Obviously your choice of jobs or career direction will be substantially different if you anticipate working only for a few months rather than years.

In reviewing a number of case histories in which the wife planned to work only a short period of time, it was found that most had seriously underestimated the time that it was necessary to work. They had settled on dead-end jobs far below their capabilities. Many had a choice between jobs and had based their choices on such factors as more money per hour or more convenient location rather than looking at long-term advantages or disadvantages. Perhaps the most important lesson learned from these experiences is that temporary is seldom temporary.

Although the emotions and the pressures involved in this type of reentry will be discussed in a later chapter, be aware at this point that realism is extremely important in assessing your reasons, your circumstances, and possible future situations. Consider your options at this point and pick the option that will offer the greatest flexibility. Use the "what-if" approach—ask yourself how you would react to several different circumstances such as income levels not meeting expectations, layoffs forcing relocation, or college expenses continuing beyond expectations. In short, it is best to approach the so-called temporary return to the work force with as much care and thought as you would a permanent return.

Worksheet: Career Planning for Involuntary Reentry—Financial Need

1. List the reasons you have increased income needs.

_____

_____

_____

_____

_____

2. How much additional income do you need and for how long?

_____

3. How much longer can you remain in your current circumstances before additional income is required?

_____

4. How would your income needs change in the event of the death of your spouse, divorce, or illness?

_____

_____

_____

5. Would you have the time and the resources to consider any type of retraining? _____

6. What types of work or positions currently interest you?

_____

_____

_____

_____

_____

7. Review your previous work history and list those skills that you previously learned that apply to your current interests.

_____

_____

_____

_____

_____

8. Considering your current interests, your income needs, and your previous skills, what job goals are realistically attainable?

Short-term: _____

_____

_____

_____

_____

Long-term: _____

_____

_____

_____

_____

Crisis or trauma   In situations involving crisis, the decision to return to the work force is completely involuntary. Your decision has been made for you because you need to eat, have a roof over your head, and pay the bills. In many cases, the situation forcing your decision is sudden. Severe emotional involvement renders you incapable of logical thought or reaction for sometimes a prolonged period of time. Case histories involving crisis show similar patterns: hopping from job to job, changing the type of job, inability to find a job, inability to cope emotionally with any type of job, blaming everything and everybody except oneself for job problems.

Divorce is by far the most prevalent reason for involuntary return to the work force—not surprising considering the current statistics on marriages that fail. The impact of divorce on a woman's ability to cope with finding employment depends largely on the amount of warning she had that her marriage was failing. Some women are able to read the handwriting on the wall far enough in advance to prepare themselves both emotionally and careerwise while others are taken completely by surprise. However, under any circumstances, divorce will result in emotions that affect preparations to reenter the job market. The only difference between one person and another is a question of degree.

Some of the following chapters will discuss the various emotions involved in involuntary reentry, because these emotions—fear, anger, anxiety, insecurity—seriously limit the effectiveness of the job search, job performance, and job satisfaction. Failing to recognize and cope with these emotions may subject you to a series of job experiences that will affect your chances for success for many years to come.

Worksheet: Career Planning for Involuntary Reentry—Crisis or Trauma

1. Review the circumstances leading to your current situation.

_____

_____

_____

2. List your current short-term needs.

_____

_____

_____

3. List your long-term goals.

_____

_____

_____

4. List your reasons for leaving your last three positions.

_____

_____

_____

5. Describe your current mental and emotional state realistically and objectively.

_____

_____

_____

_____

6. List the sources of counseling and support that would be available to you if necessary.

_____

_____

Career Change

Although it has been assumed that career change is predominately a man's issue, this assumption is becoming increasingly less accurate as more women become involved in careers rather than just jobs. Women also have considerably more choice in careers now than they have ever had before. Since they are now in many different career fields, they are subject to the same forces that have changed the labor market, particularly in the past four decades.

The term *career change* applies to a different set of circumstances than the term *job change*. In this context, a change in career means a change in direction, also implying a need for specific training or education. A job change refers to a change in unskilled positions rather than semiskilled, highly skilled, technical, or professional direction.

In the fifties and sixties, anyone who attempted to make a significant change in career direction was viewed with suspicion. In a period when a career was considered to be a life-long commitment, any changes were considered to be an admission of failure. Unfortunately, few were aware of or appreciated the massive changes that were beginning to take place in the American labor force. The dislocation of entire industries had already started. At this point, most industries were moving within the United States. Often these relocations included job transfers. Usually few, if any, unskilled or semiskilled employees were offered positions at a new location. However, highly technical, management, and executive personnel were offered the opportunity to move with the company. In fact, relocation was considered to be part of upward mobility for the young professional manager.

Many positions within career fields were disappearing as industries moved overseas, technical specialties became obsolete, and other patterns changed within the economy. Certain technical advances in electronics and data processing had the greatest impacts on job structures. This probably still is the largest component in the ever-changing job market. As a result of these massive changes, employers recognized that career change was a natural and necessary part of an employment structure in a state of constant evolution. Employers further recognized that both society and business should encourage and aid career-change individuals by retraining or cross utilizing them.

Presently, those in the process of changing careers are seldom viewed negatively. Employers now pay more attention to the reasons behind changes. Personnel and human resource staffs are trained to evaluate translatable skills, particularly when new job requirements emerge without a training mechanism to furnish adequate personnel.

Those of you considering career changes, however, share many of the same potential problems and barriers as those reentering the job marketplace. Although your experience may be recent, the question as to whether or not your experience can be translated to other careers and at what level is still critical to your success. Equally important in preparing for a career change is the identification of the reason or reasons that you are considering change because you will invariably have to explain that reason to a prospective employer, and your reason will determine the type of preparations you will have to make before starting the job search process.

The following are some of the common reasons for contemplating career changes and some of the preparations necessary for each.

Increased financial reward Money is the accepted standard or symbol of success and accomplishment, and few employees feel that they are adequately compensated. However, many feel that their inadequate compensation is not a condition that can be solved by demanding a raise or being promoted. Inadequate money is beyond the control of either themselves or their superiors. The amount of compensation is determined by factors inherent in the career field. Some examples of this type of limitation are as follows:

- The employment and the wage scales are highly structured, as in government employment and highly unionized industries.

- The specific industry is depressed, for example, the petroleum industry and heavy equipment industry.

- A portion or all of the industry has relocated, possibly overseas. This is true of the auto, electronic, and textile industries.

- The supply-and-demand characteristics of the job specialty limit compensation. In the final analysis, every job has a top limit of compensation established by supply and demand as well as the ability to contribute to profits. A significant number of those who want to change careers because of money problems simply have reached the top level of compensation for their jobs.

Career changes in this category have some decided advantages. The most important advantage is time. If you are considering change because of income level, you are probably still employed and have the opportunity to do the necessary job research and preparation without excessive pressure. Certainly many of you are currently enrolled in various types of educational or training programs as part of your overall plan to make the change.

Time is important from another viewpoint. Changing careers to obtain a greater potential income often involves starting in your new career field in a lower level position and at a lower income. Often, however, time allows you to obtain more education and experience, particularly in translatable or transferable skills, thus allowing you to make the change at higher entry levels.

Lack of challenge in your current job

Many of you have reached a plateau in your job or career field, a point that is a dead end. Your duties have become routine and boring, and you have reached the point where you actually hate to go to work. Job dissatisfaction stems from varied causes; almost every case or situation is unique. For example, one case history involves a person who had been a rehabilitation counselor for fourteen years, usually in a correctional institution. He had become dissatisfied with the position because, on the surface, he had reached a plateau in terms of both income and advancement. There was, however, another reason, perhaps not as recognizable or apparent, but one that bothered him constantly. His work environment was always completely negative and depressing. Seldom, if ever, was he aware of the positive results that he may have achieved. His interaction with other people always involved those with serious, sometimes unsolvable, problems. Increasingly he viewed his efforts as futile. The lack of any tangible evidence of accomplishment began to affect his family life. Consequently, at age thirty-seven he has made the decision to change careers,

His situation is common. After years of training and work experience, many find that either their perception of the job has changed, or the career field itself has changed. They are left occupying a position that holds neither interest nor future promise.

Current statistics confirm the fact that a significant number of people leave their chosen fields very early in their working lives, some by choice, but most probably because of the types of jobs available when they needed one.

Whatever the reason, only 25 to 30 percent have remained in the field of their training after ten years.

Many of these changes have occurred because people's actual experience in a career field does not match the expectations or concepts of the job they had while they were still in training or college.

Technical obsolescence

Looking back over the past four or five decades, it is difficult to find jobs that have not changed significantly. Technological changes have affected practically every industry. Advances in electronics, plastics, communications, computerization, and transportation have completely eliminated some industries. Overseas competition has virtually eliminated others as new plant technology provides more efficient facilities and the gap between domestic and foreign labor costs continues to widen. In some industries, changes have taken place in an orderly fashion. Employees have been allowed to adjust to the changes as they have taken place either with on-the-job training or through specialized training courses and seminars. Other industries, however, have simply disappeared or reduced their work force drastically, forcing thousands back out into the labor market.

For those of you caught in the technical obsolescence muddle, it is difficult to recognize the fact that your skills are no longer marketable despite all the warning signs— lack of promotions, continuing layoffs and declining profits. Many continue to cling to the hope that things are going to turn around, but under these circumstances it will seldom happen.

Technical obsolescence will continue to be one of the principal reasons for career change as research constantly uncovers new products and methods. Fortunately, educational and technical training facilities have been increasingly sensitive to the problem; adult retraining has become a major function of the educational system. By taking advantage of these retraining opportunities, those who heed the warning of technical obsolescence can prepare to make a change without severe dislocation or financial loss.

High unemployment in your field or locale

Localized high unemployment happens when industries or companies adjust to the marketplace. The textile industry moved South, and then much of it moved overseas. The shoe industry has relocated several times. Continued foreign competition in the auto industry has resulted in numerous areas of high unemployment throughout the United States. Faced with this problem, you have a choice of either moving to the place where the jobs in your specialty are or changing. Many of the jobs have moved overseas, leaving you with only one practical solution—making the change.

Another common cause of localized unemployment is the frequent adjustments in defense spending. Major defense contractors—such as General Electric, General Dynamics, Hughes Helicopter, and Pratt-Whitney—employ thousands in each of their locations and are often the primary employers within their geographical areas. When a major contract runs out or an anticipated contract fails to materialize, thousands of employees can be laid off. These layoffs can have a domino effect as subcontractors, retailers, and service industries also suffer cutbacks and layoffs.

Whatever the reason, high unemployment in a localized area may sometimes be temporary. However, even in situations in which the jobs return, the waiting line is usually too long for many people to survive economically.

Realistically, those of you who are involved in industries that are highly susceptible to shifts in overall economy, the defense budget, or similar forces or are in a declining industry in your area should begin planning for a second career. Even if the second career is designed only to get you over periods of temporary layoff or to provide you with greater opportunities for mobility, planning and preparation is much easier and less stressful when you are still employed. As you prepare, remember that tranferability of skills is still one of the keys.

Relocation to an area with no opportunities

Job counselors in the South, Southwest, and West are very familiar with this type of employment situation. Workers by the thousands have left the industrialized Northeast and Midwest; some are motivated by employment problems, but many are primarily seeking a change in climate and life-style. These relocatees seem to fall into two categories: those who are completely surprised by the lack of jobs in their skill areas and those who are fully aware of the lack of employment but are prepared emotionally to make a career change. Even those who are aware of the job situation often have not done enough homework to know what direction to take in their new location.

Often those with higher skills or in managerial positions have the most difficulty in adjusting to their new living and occupational environment. Their salary expectations are often higher than they can obtain; their planning for a second career is hampered by their unwillingness to accept the fact that their education and experience are not as marketable in their new location.

Some employers are also reluctant to hire people who have just relocated, particularly if extensive training or retraining is involved. They prefer to spend the money on someone they are reasonably certain will stay around long enough for training to pay off. In their perception, the newly arrived relocatee is not as good a gamble as the long-term resident.

The size of the community also determines the variety of jobs available. However, even larger cities still have an orientation toward certain types of industry. Some areas may be oriented toward heavy manufacturing, others toward high tech, tourism, financial services, or distribution. Relocatees who have not researched the occupational orientation of an area to which they plan to move may have a rude awakening when they first look for employment.

If you fall into this category or think you do, a visit to the local state employment office should be your first priority. It will have information and statistics concerning the number of jobs existing in every job category. If you are one of those whose skills are not marketable in a certain area, the faster you know that a career change is necessary, the faster you can start the process. Unfortunately, many people spin their wheels for months looking for non-existent jobs before they finally face reality.

Consistent lack of success   There is probably no reliable data on how many round pegs have been placed in square holes as far as occupations are concerned. Anyone in personnel interviewing or counseling will attest to the fact that the number is disturbingly high. It is easy to understand how this can happen. Since World War II, there have been increasing pressures on sixteen- to eighteen-year-olds to make a career commitment. Even before graduation from high school, this age category is pressured into making the choice between college preparatory, general, or vocational courses. Upon graduation, a choice then must be made between going to work, pursuing a technical education, or deciding upon a college or university. A student's choice of college involves at least a partial commitment to a general career field. One would not go, for example, to a liberal arts college to pursue a career related to engineering. Once in college, the choice of a major must be made before the end of the second year. Considering the complexity of the job market, the vast number of different occupational specialties, and the limited opportunity for exposure to these specialties, it is safe to assume that few people have been in a position to make an intelligent choice of careers.

Many people job hop from one field to another before finally settling upon a direction that results in success and satisfaction. Many others, however, follow a history of jobs in one field without any notable success. Often the reluctance to change fields has been a matter of necessity, not of choice. Early family responsibilities, large financial commitments, lack of alternative opportunity, and geographical location are just a few of the circumstances that can limit a person trying to find the right career or job. Consequently, many people who have doubts about their own self-worth, lack the confidence to take the necessary risks, or doubt their abilities are, in reality, round pegs in a square hole.

If you even suspect that you may fall into this category, the sooner you make the change, the better. One of the most difficult classifications of career changers are the people who in their mid-forties have come to the realization that they hate what they have been doing for the past twenty years. People have different aptitudes and abilities; if you have a past history of failure in one area, it is probably because you have locked yourself into a specialty for which you have little aptitude or even interest. Very simply, if you hate to go to work in the morning, it's time to take a hard introspective look at where you are going.

An intentional plan to alter your life

Often people desire to change careers for reasons totally unrelated to the career or job itself. A career change may be only part of an effort to completely change every aspect of a person's life-style. A desire for change can be motivated by some personal trauma or crisis. Divorce, death of a spouse, or abandonment usually involve not only a career change but also a change of location, life-style, and even dress. Some men and women in this category successfully complete all aspects of their change and are interested in upgrading their new career. Others are still in the beginning stages—unemployed or changing jobs continuously. Some complete the transition in less than a year while others have not yet made the adjustment after five to seven years. To some, their career is a source of stability. Their new jobs become an important part of their new life; in fact, many attribute their personal adjustment to their job.

Others seem to use their employment as a scapegoat for all their pent-up anger and frustration, blaming bosses, co-workers, and working conditions for their failures and their job hopping.

Almost without exception, the phrase *getting my head on straight* is used to describe this period of adjustment. Even those who have not yet made the adjustment know that this act is a critical part of the adjustment process. By paying particular attention to the part played by a job or career, several trends become apparent.

- Those who appear most satisfied are those whose second career appears successful.

- Those who look at another job as merely a matter of putting a roof over their head instead of looking for something that would satisfy personal or ego needs are those who seem most unhappy, maladjusted, and dissatisfied with their personal situation. As one woman, now a successful property manager, said, "I spent the first three years after my divorce going from one job to another hoping that I was going to find Mr. Perfect and return to my former life-style. I finally stopped looking long enough to take stock of my situation and realized that I was making the same mistake that I made in my first marriage—putting all my eggs in one basket. I was looking again to invest all my financial and emotional rewards on one person and becoming as vulnerable as I was during my first marriage. It was then and only then that I looked for more than money in my choice of a job. Although at this point I am involved in a relationship, it shares my life with my career rather than dominating me."

- Many case histories involve people who have not yet decided on the direction for a second career even after several years. In most cases, the principal reasons for the lack of decision involve emotions left from the crisis—fear, anxiety, and anger. These emotions are hampering them in making many critical decisions. In most cases they are aware that they are still in a transitional stage and have a way to go before they "have their heads on straight."

  On the opposite side of the coin, some are not aware that the emotions related to their personal traumas are severely affecting their ability to make decisions and to objectively evaluate both their own skills and availability and the job opportunities and conditions within their job market. Typically, people in this category devote considerable time during pre-employment and employment interviews discussing their personal life or recounting how successful they were before "it" happened. They pay little attention to questions asked by the interviewer and do not organize either their presentations or their responses. In short, they talk endlessly and compulsively.

• Those for whom a job has been a stabilizing factor during a traumatic period funnel most of their energies and time into the job. The job has to furnish elements of ego satisfaction, involve them with other people, and require both concentration and continuing commitment. It is important to realize that menial and repetitive jobs requiring little involvement and commitment offer little help or focus to those going through a personal crisis. Consequently, these types of jobs are of little value as an adjustment mechanism.

Retirement: normal, early, or forced

Despite recent legislation advancing the mandatory retirement age, people continue to retire earlier. In most cases, these early retirees attempt to remain in the labor force at least on a part-time basis. Military and many government retirement plans enable people to retire in their forties or early fifties. A second career is usually necessary from both a financial and emotional standpoint.

Forced early retirement is often the result of industry or company relocation, cutback, or closing because of competition or obsolescence. Often a company will offer long-term employees the opportunity to take an early retirement rather than a layoff, thus reducing the impact of unemployment compensation claims.

Accidents or illness often cause people to become partially disabled and thus unable to continue in their line of work. In many of these cases, the person is capable of performing work of a less strenuous or exacting nature. For example, one case involves a forty-seven-year-old man who had worked in construction for most of his life. After two minor heart attacks, the doctor advised him to go into something requiring less physical exertion. He attended drafting school and is now working as a draftsman, preparing working drawings for the construction industry.

Obviously timing is the major issue in cases involving early retirement, whether forced or planned. If you are in an occupation with a well-defined retirement system and you know when you plan to retire, the preparation and planning for your second career can be started at any time. Some military retirees prepare for their second career five or more years before their retirement date. Those retired because of company problems usually have little time to prepare or plan. If you fall into this category, you are faced with the same problem as anyone who is unexpectedly out of a job. Your only possible advantage is your retirement income, even though it may be inadequate.

Turning a hobby into a career

A significant number of you who are converting a hobby into a career are accomplishing your goals through entrepreneurship—starting your own business.

However, the focus here is on those of you with an established hobby who are trying to find a position within that field. Several examples fit this category precisely: a weekend flyer trying to find a position as a corporate pilot, an amateur artist trying to break into the graphics field, a fledgling writer who now writes newsletters but wants to become a fiction writer.

The challenge facing most people searching for a position involving skills learned as a hobby is the creation of a résumé and an interview presentation that will convince a prospective employer to take this experience seriously. Unfortunately, many employers still adhere to the thought that only paid experience is significant.

In this chapter, most of the reasons that people seek a change have been outlined. Practically every reason involves some type of emotional circumstances; in fact, change itself is an emotion-charged event. Before we begin to discuss the mechanics of the job search, we must first discuss the emotions involved in changing careers or reentering the workplace. In your type of situation, emotional preparation is critical to success. In the following chapters, we will investigate the common emotions involved with change and explain how to turn these emotions into positive forces helping you make the changes.

Career change worksheets

The following worksheets are designed to allow you to put your thoughts about making a career change on paper. Sometimes, if not always, writing about your thoughts forces you to be more realistic and more introspective, giving you something tangible to reflect upon.

Worksheet: Job-Related Causes for Career Change

Job-related reasons for considering career change can be classified as either voluntary or involuntary. Identifying your true reason for wishing to change career direction can be very helpful in determining your options in terms of time and preparation. As you fill in the information requested below, remember that everyone has the tendency to rationalize dissatisfaction or failure. Be as realistic and honest as possible in your responses.

Voluntary Reasons for Career Change

Increased financial reward

1. Why is your income below your expectations or goal?

_____

_____

_____

_____

_____

2. What action or circumstances would be necessary for you to reach your goal?

_____

_____

_____

_____

3. Are you limited by highly structured wage scales, a depressed industry, an industry that has relocated, or the fact that you have reached the top level of compensation for your job? If so, which one?

_____

_____

_____

_____

Lack of challenge in your current job

1. Why are you dissatisfied with your current position?

_____

_____

_____

_____

2. What must occur to make your job equal your expectations?

_____

_____

_____

_____

3. Realistically, what are the chances that the required changes can or will occur?

_____

_____

_____

Involuntary Reasons for Career Change

Technical obsolescence

1. What changes have taken place in your current field?

_____

_____

_____

_____

2. Are these changes industrywide or just in your local area?

_____

3. Is change of locale an option for you? _____

4. Are there retraining or skill-upgrading opportunities available to you? If so, at what expense in terms of money and time?

_____

_____

_____

_____

5. Are any of your current skills transferrable to other fields? If so, what skills can you transfer? To what fields?

_____

_____

_____

_____

_____

_____

_____

High unemployment in your field or locale

1. Do you consider the high employment rate in your area to be temporary or permanent? Why?

_____

_____

_____

_____

2. If an upturn is possible, can you afford, in terms of both time and money, to wait for it to happen? Why?

_____

_____

_____

3. Is moving to where the jobs in your field are an option?

_____

Relocation to an area with no opportunities

1. Were you aware of the employment situation when you relocated?

_____

2. Did you intend to change careers after relocating?

_____

3. If you did not intend to change careers, do you now consider a change to be your only option? If not, what other options do you have?

_____

_____

_____

_____

_____

Consistent lack of success

1. List below the three jobs that you would most enjoy at this stage of your life. Use your imagination.

    a. _____

    b. _____

    c. _____

2. In what basic ways do these positions differ from your current field?

_____

_____

_____

_____

3. Are any of your current skills applicable to the three jobs you would most enjoy?

_____

_____

4. List the most disagreeable aspects of your current position.

_____

_____

_____

_____

_____

5. List the most positive aspects of your current position.

_____

_____

_____

_____

_____

6. Review the three positions chosen previously and determine how many of the pluses and minuses of your current position are found in the three you have chosen.

Job A _____

_____

_____

Job B _____

_____

_____

Job C _____

_____

_____

7. Based on your answers above, do you feel that you are in the career field that you are most qualified and suited for?

_____

Retirement: normal, early, or forced

1. Are you emotionally and financially prepared to retire?

_____

2. If not, why do you *not* want to try to find a position in your previous career field?

_____

_____

3. How much longer do you plan to work full-time?

_____

_____

4. What income level is necessary to sustain your previous life-style?

_____

5. Considering that this change will probably be your last career, what aspects of your new career do you feel are most important?

_____

_____

_____

The Emotions of Change

2

Change is usually threatening—or at least unsettling—to all of us. It means facing the unknown, leaving the familiar. It can produce feelings of fear and anxiety; it can shake our confidence levels. However, change can also be stimulating, inspiring, refreshing, and filled with promise. These positive aspects of change emerge eventually. However, they are less likely to surface immediately when change is forced upon us or brought about by a crisis in our personal lives. Crisis can cause the need for many changes simultaneously and sometimes in drastic measure. The emotions normally brought about by change are then heightened. Our view of the situation can be distorted. As the person most directly involved, you can feel as if you are failing, being abandoned, and left entirely alone. There is a sense of having nowhere and no one to turn to.

This is especially true for persons going through crisis that stems from the loss of a marriage partner, whether it be from death or divorce. Under these circumstances, it is difficult to think clearly about very much. Your emotions are more in control than you are. It is often painful to sort out your feelings, even more painful to make practical plans for the future. You may not see that you have alternatives because your needs are so immediate. With all of this churning inside you, it is next to impossible to be decisive about anything, much less a future career.

For those of you who are making this change by choice because you have recognized a need to do so, there may be some distinct advantages. You may have the time to think and plan for this change. It is something you wish to do, and you may experience positive feelings. But even then the emotions that are caused by change itself can still create some very stressful and strained times. Always there is the moment of decision that must be reached and faced, for that is what the process is all about.

This chapter is dedicated to the emotions that are most troublesome to us when we are faced with change and the decision process. These emotions can be found in one degree or another in both females and males. They often exist whether a person is planning changes of reentry, of career, or of moving on to an entrepreneurship and whether changes are brought about by choice or by need.

Fear

Each of us has certainly known fear throughout our lives. We have each learned to cope with this emotion one way or another. Fear can provoke physical symptoms such as raising our blood pressure, making our heart pound, making us sick to our stomach, or gripping us with cold chills. There are many more documented reactions of the physical nature of fear. Fear has its psychological effects as well. Fear can distort reality and undo our reasoning powers. It can stimulate other feelings such as those of panic, of being threatened, or of being intimidated.

A way to cope

Many of these reactions occur in our defense. They allow us to deal with only the amount of fear we are capable of handling at this time. They are our coping mechanism. Some persons take a firm and stubborn stand against their fears while others are willed into taking flight (taking off in another direction or making a complete retreat) away from the object of fear. That is the theory of *fight or flight.*

We as individuals find our own most effective way of coping with our fear response.

Not only does each of us have our own response to fear but we also have our own list of what is fear producing and a very personalized system with which we rate the level or degree to which we are threatened by it. So what is perhaps only moderately stressful to one person may well be terribly frightening to another.

Analyzing fear   In examining your own fear-producing situations, try not to be judgmental toward yourself. Accept that these are part of your uniqueness. It will be helpful if you begin by making a list of what you are most fearful of in your present situation. Include the little things as well as the major ones. Some of the fears which weave a common theme are those of failure. Failure includes failing to find a job, a good job, the "right" job, an exceptional job. Some people never are able to move to the point of making a definite decision or a firm commitment toward anything specific. They become hung in limbo, fearful they will take the "wrong" job and later regret it. Mostly they are afraid there might be something even better out there waiting for them. Some who have made career changes before feel they settled for something that did not make them happy or for some reason did not work out. They are afraid of making the same mistake again.

Some people fear they will fail to perform once they have obtained a job. Perhaps the job will be too big for them, the responsibilities too awesome. Along with this is also the fear of failing to get along with co-workers or be liked, accepted, and respected by them. This is particularly evident in persons who have either been out of the work force for an extended period of time or who have had unfortunate experiences in the past. These persons are fearful of making themselves vulnerable to the same situation again. Some have fears of being able to maintain the pace or meet the time demands of a new career. Sometimes these fears are legitimate.

In the processes of both reentry and career change, there are fears of the unknown. Not only do people have concern for making the right career choice, but at what level of the new career they will need to start? If a salary cut is necessary, can they manage on less? For how long will that be necessary? Heads of households particularly fear they will be placing an additional burden on their family by making these changes. Where relocation is also involved, there is concern—if not outright fear—of how well the family unit will survive the move and readjustment to a new environment.

Reentry people have a common set of fears stemming from being out of the work force for numerous years. They fear that their skills and education are not current. Many fear that they do not have enough education to compete for the jobs they desire. Many have interrupted their educations to marry and have children. It seems these women are often fearful that their life experiences will not be considered valuable. Since they have had no recent paid employment, how can they expect to compete with younger people for the position of their choice? Many have already accepted that they will need to return to school to update or complete an education, but that is no less frightening. Again, the chore of trying to compete with younger students is a major factor.

Along that same thread of thought are the obvious fears associated with rejection due to age and sex. Discrimination is illegal, but it exists, and it affects both males and females. There is another age issue. Some people fear that time is running out or is too limited to allow them success, at least to the level of their aspirations.

Fear comes in many shapes and sizes. Examine yours. Make your list.

Anxiety

Fear generates anxiety, an uneasiness over an impending unknown. When you have completed your list of fears, see how they will affect your future hopes. For instance, if you are fearful of how competent you are in reentering the work force, write down all the reasons you feel incompetent. If you're planning to return to a type of work you did previously, are you anxious about changes that have occurred in your absence such as in equipment, procedures, or new information? Look seriously at what it would require for you to become current. Does your anxiety stem from the recognition that you will need to take a refresher course or return to school? Perhaps that in itself is a fear, or perhaps it appears to be an impossibility.

An example of this is one woman who put aside the completion of her education in order to marry and to then stay home with her children. Periodically she would take a class and always enjoyed doing so. She felt perfectly capable of returning to school, but following a divorce, she became very anxious about doing so. She knew it was not because she feared school itself, but she was terribly anxious about spending the time and money doing so. Her finances were already strained, her energy drained; she rationalized that school would take additional time away from her children. She later came to realize that her underlying reason was guilt. Going to school meant that she was doing something for herself, using resources for her personal gain. Because of feelings the divorce had left her with, she simply felt unworthy.

Readjustment anxieties

Women who have worked at home for a number of years are generally anxious about how this will affect their job situation. Some feel that those years are wasted or will count for nothing. Or they feel that the years out of the work force will put them behind their contemporaries as far as salaries, benefits, and even promotions and responsibilities are concerned. They question whether it will ever be possible for them to catch up or compete on equal ground. For the most part, these women also express fears about whether they will also be able to manage everything and everyone they have left in the home. For these women, reentering the work force is not an easy adjustment, especially if there is no solid support coming from other family members.

Image anxieties

On a more personal level, many are anxious about their own image. These worries include whether their wardrobe, hairstyle, or body image fit those of a working woman. One woman searched through her closets trying to find something to wear that seemed appropriate for an interview. Over the years she had worn sportswear during the day, and the rest of her clothing was for dress-up occasions. She had known from the start that she was not financially able to purchase new clothing to start a job hunt or to begin a job. This was a real concern for her and definitely anxiety producing.

Interview anxieties

Interviews can make anyone anxious. Dissatisfaction with your weight or your looks for any reason will only lower your self-confidence and further raise your anxiety level. For those making a reentry, there is often concern over how they will be able to handle themselves in the interview situation. It may seem as if you have forgotten how to talk with people. And if one of your fears is how your co-workers will accept you, then it follows that this will also be a worry connected with your image and how you'll appear to the people you will meet and work with.

Changing careers may also mean changing attitudes, professional lingo, and method of doing things. Working with a small group of people and joining a large group, or vice versa, will require adjustment. Becoming a new member of any group can be very stressful for many people.

Worksheet: Dealing with Fear and Anxiety

My Fears

Most stressful:

1. _____
   _____
   _____

2. _____
   _____
   _____

3. _____
   _____
   _____

4. _____
   _____
   _____

5. _____
   _____
   _____

My Coping Mechanisms

I can cope with this fear by:

1. _____
   _____
   _____

2. _____
   _____
   _____

3. _____
   _____
   _____

4. _____
   _____
   _____

5. _____
   _____
   _____

Anxiety

How these fears could affect my plans for the future:

Fear #1 _____

_____

_____

_____

_____

Fear #2 _____

_____

_____

_____

_____

Fear #3 _____

_____

_____

_____

_____

Fear #4 _____

_____

_____

_____

_____

Fear #5 _____

_____

_____

_____

_____

Anger
This is a common but intriguing emotion. Throughout the paths of people's changes, they often express anger in one form or another. This is equally true of persons making career changes by choice and of those who feel they are forced to make a change. Some persons have no problem recognizing their anger and are able to describe who and what their anger has been directed at. Others either do not recognize their feelings as anger or are too uncomfortable to label the emotion as anger. All the same, in most instances it is there. That is why you will be encouraged to look for yours if you are not already aware of its presence. Complete the worksheet on page 37. In one column write why you are angry. In the next column put who or what it seems to be focused on.

Reasons for anger
Each of us has all kinds of reasons for the *why* category. These will be very personal and extremely individual. You need not share this list with anyone else, so you can be very open and honest with it. Having a long list does not mean you are a horrible person either. It probably means you are really willing to identify things that until now you have only been stuffing away as hurts or grudges. We all have these; most of us manage to file them away in the hope that they will just go away. That is often not the case. Instead, the next time something happens that reminds us of it, there is a flashback effect. As we continue to stuff away, the little file just gets fuller. When it gets too full, there is a "fallout."

Things that make you angry
The *what* category appears to evolve mostly out of situations or things that happen that are not of our making or within our control. Some examples include layoffs, illnesses, or relocations due to someone else's plan. Sudden and unexpected layoffs seem totally unjustified, especially when you are being told what a fine job you are doing for the company. This was the case of one man. In the case of another, the system he worked for merely disbanded without warning.

People who make you angry
Anger directed at a *who* seems to fit into three groups: others, family, and self. Examples of others are those corporations or school systems that have so very impersonally determined the individual's fate. This group also includes

more broad, less definable things like the changing job market, the rising unemployment rate, changing technology, society's nonrecognition of life skills, or the expectations or lack of understanding of peer groups.

When anger is directed at family, the most frequent target is a spouse or former spouse. The most common cause for crisis is divorce. Often a divorce precipitates the need for change or reentry. In many instances anger can be intertwined with the reasons for divorce as well as being directed toward a spouse. However, that is not always the case. One women was angry with her husband because, as her children grew more independent, she wished to go back to work outside their home. Her husband did not want her to do so. This woman finally followed her own judgement and found a job, but she tried to maintain the family's lifestyle as if nothing had changed. She had not anticipated any help with the household chores. Even under these conditions, her husband refused to adjust to the new arrangement and, of course, offered her no emotional support or approval. She was angry. Their marriage did eventually end in divorce. Following that, she could fully recognize her anger.

People who are angry with themselves often generate feelings of failure. They can find plenty of reasons to justify those feelings. If they are divorced, they feel they have failed at a marriage.

If their children aren't helpful around the house, they feel they have failed as a parent. Crisis, fear, and anger can uncover all sorts of frustrations and disappointments which we may see as being of our own making. Women who have voluntarily given up careers to work at home for many years can become particularly vulnerable to this way of thinking. If they are fearful of what those years may cost them in the job market, they can become very angry with themselves for being taken in by that decision, though at the time it was a conscious decision. They therefore have no one to blame but themselves, right? And there is another kind of blaming that goes on by both men and women who are unhappy with their body images. They can be very angry for "letting themselves go," wondering how they ever allowed themselves to get this out of shape, overweight, or mentally lazy.

Anger directed at self is not any more justified than anger directed at other sources. One case study was a male who had had a successful series of jobs. For years he continued to grow professionally and financially, always moving ahead and in the directions he chose. Suddenly the career he was developing came to an absolute halt for reasons totally out of his control. When he was asked about the anger he felt toward those individuals who had eliminated the possibility of that career for him, he stated that he was not angry with them. He thought he had accepted the whole major setback very philosophically. What he had actually done was direct his anger at himself, and as proof, he set himself up for more disappointments and failure.

You've heard the saying about how wonderful hindsight can be. It is also a fantastic tool for blaming yourself if you are not careful. Blaming can be a game we play with ourselves to keep us from identifying anger.

Worksheet: Analyzing Anger

Why I'm angry: **Who/what the anger is focused on:**

1. _____   _____

   _____   _____

   _____   _____

2. _____   _____

   _____   _____

   _____   _____

3. _____   _____

   _____   _____

   _____   _____

4. _____   _____

   _____   _____

   _____   _____

5. _____   _____

   _____   _____

   _____   _____

Lack of Self-Confidence

Confidence in ourselves—self-confidence—is often a mirrored effect of what social programming has led us to believe we should be. We may adapt the standards of our society as expectations or goals by which we measure our self-worth. When we do not feel we are meeting expectations or attaining goals, it can have an eroding effect on our level of self-confidence.

Social standards

Social standards are changing, but ever so slowly. Paid work experience is still regarded as more valuable than unpaid experience. This leaves the volunteer and housewife in a less desirable position. And there is still a prevailing attitude that women do not take their careers as seriously as do men and that interruptions are to be expected. Unfortunately, women are still paid less in the positions they hold than are men. Clearly these social standards have a great effect on the confidence levels of women, and especially on those making a reentry into the job market.

Our society has become very credential oriented. The need for increased educational levels and degrees is a reality. Government regulations, licensing, and upgrading of requirements are in part responsible for the required additional credentials. The nation's economy dictates the employment rate and growth. In a tight job market, emphasis on these credentials increases even more. In making a reentry or career change, whether you have the expected credentials strongly influences your self-confidence.

Crisis and self-confidence

On a purely emotional level, all our fears, anxieties—even our anger—play a part in how we see ourselves and judge our worth. What we present to the world is how we think "they" will judge us. Self-doubt and questioning our self-worth are prevalent during a state of crisis. If we feel uncertain of our capabilities, unprepared to take on new responsibilities, unable to deal with all the changes, we are almost certain to fail in accomplishing our desired goal. Failing decreases self-confidence, and we can set up a vicious cycle.

Reentry people are most lacking in self-confidence. This can be expected. One woman felt that she had vegetated during the years she had remained at home. Another felt as if she had been a "nonperson" for so long she wasn't sure who she was anymore. Most feel they are starting from ground zero in their preparations. Those making career changes feel confident in the area of their past performance and think their past work records are good. But they are not necessarily confident this will carry them through the transition into a new career. They recall what it was like when they started the first career.

By definition, crisis is a turning point, which means we must take a new direction and most probably leave a good deal of the familiar behind. Coping with change can be exhausting. Crisis in our personal lives can trigger exaggerated feelings of inadequacy. A career change can mean starting over, unless the new career is similar to a former one. Any time we assume we are moving backward instead of forward with our goals, our self-image and self-confidence will be lowered.

If relocation is also a part of the change, a person can suddenly be left without the former contacts, support systems, and recognition and prestige gained from those former associates and peers. Your past is a blank. You cannot transfer the goodwill of others from your past endeavors. What you bring along with you is what can be written down in a reference, and it is not the same. One man felt very alone and very much on the outside. In his down moments, he questioned whether he had read those former support systems correctly—whether he had merely imagined his previous popularity—and his self-doubts grew.

Feeling uninformed can also wear away your self-confidence, especially when you are certain everyone else is informed. Those making reentry have not generally stayed current with salary schedules and benefits. They may find themselves totally unprepared to discuss salary expectations, choices of insurance plans, tax consequences, and investment programs. There are at least a dozen-and-one situations that can feed your feelings of inadequacy, which in turn will foster the lowering of your confidence level.

If you have been able to identify with any or all of these emotions, let us assure you that you are not alone. Most people going through change have experienced these emotions to some degree. Let us also reassure you that these feelings are in no way abnormal, and they are temporary.

The emotions of fear, anxiety, anger, and low self-esteem can have a seriously limiting effect on the decision-making process and job search. These emotional effects can be extended to job performance and job satisfaction as well. If you are experiencing crisis in your personal life, you may be so absorbed by these emotions that your judgment may be impaired. Your ability to make clear, concise decisions can be hampered as we saw in several case studies. Your job search is made more difficult because you are not representing yourself at your best. Even after you have secured a job, your emotions may still be controlling your life, and there may be little relief from the negative aspects of these feelings. Dissatisfaction soon follows. Then there may be a return to square one, time to find something else that will be "better." Frequent job changes may become a repetitive pattern. It is necesary for us to recognize and work through our emotional states, or they will become traps for us. Suggestions on how you may attempt to do this will be made in following chapters.

Worksheet: Raising Your Self-Confidence

A. List five areas in which you lack self-confidence.

1. _____
2. _____
3. _____
4. _____
5. _____

B. What can you do to raise your level of self-confidence in these areas?

1. _____
_____
_____
_____
_____

2. _____
_____
_____
_____
_____

3. _____
_____
_____
_____
_____

4. _____
_____
_____
_____
_____

5. _____
_____
_____
_____

Taking Stock of Your Skills

Have you ever been in a situation where you have been asked point blank to describe yourself or to state your strengths and weaknesses? If so, you may have experienced the same mental block so many of us do. These questions do not seem to be so difficult. The answers should be fairly obvious since we know ourselves better than anyone else, right? Wrong. Even when we do know the answers to these questions, most of us are hesitant to answer. We fear if we answer too quickly we may appear immodest or overconfident, giving the wrong impression, or worse, sounding conceited. That is, of course, if we do have a fairly good opinion of ourselves.

Sometimes the mental block is truly there. Our thoughts are blank. We have spent our entire lives with ourselves, yet we seem to have spent very little time thinking about ourselves in these terms. Often the first things that come to mind, and the easiest ones to state, are those things we do not like about ourselves or see as weaknesses. Many of us are not dedicated to thinking positively about ourselves and our assets, which are commonly known by those who associate with us. Indeed, it is time to take stock of yourself and to learn what you have going for you.

Since each of us is a one-of-a-kind individual, no two of us will have the same talents or skills. Even if our experiences are similar, we will not have taken the same things from them. What many of us fail to recognize is that to get where we are in life, we have had to use or develop skills that have seemed natural or unimportant in the larger scheme of things. In reality, these skills may be valuable tools in the job market. The challenge of this chapter is to take your individuality into account, to dare to be different. Discover yourself; let those creative juices flow. Put that imagination to work. Don't be afraid to flaunt your talents or explore your specialties.

While this is not the time to be shy or modest about your talents and accomplishments, there is one word of caution. Do be honest with yourself. You are exploring and rediscovering, but exaggerating what you find will do no good. Let your honesty keep your perspective but not daunt your aspirations.

Positives and Negatives

Here we are back to making lists. On the worksheet that appears on page 46, fill in the two columns: positives and negatives. Start by using free association of thoughts about yourself. As you think of a talent, skill, habit, or experience, place it in one column or the other. Don't think too long about each, but go with your first reaction. You will be adding to and changing these lists frequently, and don't be surprised if you find some of these items bouncing from one column to the other. That's perfectly all right.

Be creative, daring, and exercise your imagination a bit. The longer and more explicit these lists are, the more you will discover about yourself. Be sure to include the areas in which you feel you perform well and those with which you feel you have problems. An example would be reading. If you like to read and you are a rapid reader, you will most likely place that in the positive column, but if you either do not enjoy reading or you feel you read very slowly, then you may place that as a negative factor. Communication skills would be another example. Do you enjoy meeting people? How well do you feel you do it? Keep in mind you are looking for your strengths and weaknesses.

You will want to include your likes and dislikes, as they certainly will have an effect on your job performance. For instance, if you do not like to travel, then you would not want to take a position where it would be required on a regular basis.

Include the things you really enjoy doing or really like about yourself. Look for the positive. Be sure you include the things others appear to like about you too. If you really feel bold, you may want to enlist the help of someone you feel very close to or trust to give you reliable feedback.

Look back over the lists you made from chapter 2. Check to see if any of those emotions and the problems you are having with them should be included in either of these columns. The ones that are still troublesome to you will undoubtedly end up being negative factors. Those with which you are feeling more comfortable could well be additions to your positive list, as they may now be definite strengths. Not all fears, anxieties, or anger need be negative. Some are very useful, just as we've learned that some forms of stress actually help people perform better. It will be interesting to see how you categorize yours. As you revise your lists, you may put more thought into them and take a broader view of the issues involved. For example, if you have been directing anger at yourself for feeling as if you have wasted the last five years—either at home or on a "going-nowhere" job—you might first place the wasted time in your negative column. However, as your enthusiasm for change builds and your perspective grows, it's possible you could start thinking of those years not as wasted but as necessary to create the incentive for making a change at all. You may come to realize that without those years you would not have felt the need strongly enough to try what you have always wanted to do.

What Have You Done with Your Life?

This list should be fun. Just what have you done with your life up to this point in time? How have you spent the majority of your time? This will, of course, include previous job experiences, volunteer experiences, hobbies, activities, interests, sports, and so on. With this list we will uncover the skills you have gained through your involvement.

Managing a home and children may seem irrelevant outside the boundaries of the family, but they are not. One can acquire skills in patience, flexibility, and organization. One learns how to set priorities, do basic budgeting, finance, and material management. Crisis intervention, communication, and a host of other skills are developed by this work experience. Even free time can become useful. Some women have started craft shops on the knowledge they gathered about materials and media from their own hobbies.

Many a career has been set in motion through experiences gained as a volunteer. One woman was stimulated into starting her own secretarial and printing business after spending years as a volunteer secretary. She was sure she could manage an office better than any of the people she had worked under, and she already knew the business. Another woman admitted she was able to accept her first reentry job as a teacher's aide because she realized she had worked with children for many years by being involved in her children's group activities.

In career changes, we have frequently seen a step-building process. One young woman is a good example. She claims she was career oriented during her high school years but never focused on anything specific. After a number of jobs, she was employed by a financial institution. She continued to work there after her marriage, even though she began to feel very "dead ended." A crisis in her husband's job prompted them to relocate to another area of the country. There she found it difficult to find a job at first. Finally she found one similar to the one she had left in another financial institution. At that time she decided to return to school. Neither her husband nor her family supported her in this endeavor, but she did complete an associate degree in banking and finance. Though she had planned to continue until she earned her baccalaureate degree, due to circumstances and family pressures, she did not. Following a divorce, her education again became a priority. At this time she did return to school.

One of her first courses included a process of evaluating goals and career directions. Through this she decided to change from banking and finance to public relations. As her classes continued, she found areas in which banking and public relations crossed over, and she readily took her new skills back to her job and put them to use. She soon found her employer giving her additional responsibilities geared to her increased knowledge and skills. In essence, she had begun to gain some practical experience in her new career that she would build on to make the transition. From the financial institution, she had made some valuable contacts that she felt could be beneficial if she were to continue to work in that area, combining her job experience with her additional education credentials. She is now in the process of searching for a public relations position within the industry of banking and finance.

Worksheet: Taking Stock of Assets and Liabilities

My Positive Traits

_____

_____

_____

_____

_____

_____

_____

_____

_____

My Negative Traits

_____

_____

_____

_____

_____

_____

_____

_____

_____

What I've Done with My Life Thus Far:

Personal experiences:

_____

_____

_____

_____

Job experiences:

_____

_____

_____

_____

Volunteer experiences:

_____

_____

_____

_____

Hobbies:

_____

_____

_____

_____

Sports:

_____

_____

_____

_____

Crafts:

_____

_____

_____

_____

Other interests:

_____

_____

_____

Realities Sooner or later we must return to basics. By this time you should have done some serious thinking about what you must do (that is, make a change), what your capabilities are, and what direction you are interested in taking. Next, you need to know what will be required of you to make this change.

If you have a fairly good idea of what you would like to develop as a career, then you probably already know what credentials are necessary to attain it. If not, it's time for investigation. You can do this through employment counseling, placement agencies, books, or even by calling the personnel departments offering the type of jobs you are looking for. Don't just stop with learning the academic requirements. Make inquiries as to what personal qualities, skills, previous experience, and other prerequisites employers are looking for. If there does not seem to be specific information available, rely on some common sense to fill in some of the blanks. For instance, if you are interested in a career in marketing, it would seem reasonable to expect that the position would require the ability to meet people easily, to organize your own time, to be able to sell a product or service, and in most instances, to provide your own transportation for business calls.

After learning all you can about what will be required to attain a job and then to perform on it, look at your own credentials, both educational and job related. Do this by using your lists of positive and negative factors and experiences. Hopefully you will be pleasantly surprised to find that they interrelate. Don't expect to find a perfect match, however, but watch for those that become transferable.

Often women who are reentering the job force are also making a career change. The reasons seem fairly obvious. Many of them did not start a career before they married and began to have children. Others held jobs but were not thinking in terms of careers. Still others began a career but set it aside when their children were born. Years later, when they either chose to return to the outside work force or were compelled to do so by circumstances, they found their former type of employment inappropriate or insufficient to meet their new needs. Women who had been qualified in professions such as teaching or nursing found drastic changes had occurred in those professions during their years of absence. Many also found that their credentials and education needed updating.

A change of careers can be equally trying for those who are making a switch from one field of endeavor to another. It may require retraining in the form of a totally new set of knowledge and skills. Such was the case of one woman who left the military, where she was working in a chaplaincy program. As a civilian, she chose to enter the field of property management. Others who make career changes may require new knowledge but find their former skills still applicable. This was true for a man who made the change from a position as a field manager of sales for a corporation to becoming a realtor. During his years with the corporation, he had gained a lot of experience with sales. Those skills were transferable to real estate, even though the product was vastly different as were the credential requirements. It meant he had to return to an educational program in order to obtain his realtor's license.

If this appears to be true for your situation, that some skills are transferable but others are needed, then there is another area of reality that you should explore. This includes time and finances. Gaining academic credits requires both. Determine just what your time frame is for making this change. If you can afford the time, what about the financial aspects? Explore the possibilities of working and going back to school at the same time. Many find that their financial limitations require them to do it this way.

Both time and finances could limit the careers that are feasible for you to seek. The head of a household, newly laid off or relocated, does not have the same options as another person who considers retirement and then chooses a career change instead. Other responsibilities play into time and finances too. One single woman did not have time to receive further education before she was forced to return to work following a divorce. She had two minor children to parent and partially support. She had a mortgage payment to meet. All these demands strained finances and limited time. Then there was an additional concern for her children's adjustment to the divorce. She felt she needed every extra ounce of energy to cope with that situation. Not only were her career choices limited, but her decision had to be an immediate one.

Worksheet: Realities

1. Credentials I'll need: _____

_____

2. Time it may take to earn these credentials: _____

_____

3. Finances:

    A. Funds available for further education: _____

    B. The amount I still need: _____

    C. My financial restraints will be: _____

    _____

    _____

4. Previous job experiences that will be required in my new career:

_____

_____

5. Transferable skills I have: _____

_____

_____

6. Personal qualities that will be useful in my new career: _____

_____

_____

7. Time restraints: _____

_____

_____

8. Other responsibilities that must be considered in my decision are: _____

_____

_____

Decision   Ultimately a decision must be reached. The lists you have formed and the investigations you have made are tools. Check your facts, tally your lists, and then move on to the final step in the decision-making process: decide on something. Even a decision not to make a career change at this point will be a valid decision. If you do not have the luxury of deciding to continue with the familiar and are forced to make a change, then what it will be is up to you. When you will do it and how you will do it are part of that decision. Don't stop in the middle of the process. Make the decision as clear as you possibly can so that you will be ready to move on to the next steps with a sense of progress.

Following your decision, you will be able to set goals for yourself and establish a time frame in which to work toward them. Neither goals nor time frames need to be cast in cement—they will probably be more helpful if they have some flexibility built into them. If they are realistic and reasonable, there is less probability of having to make major adjustments to them. For your own sake, take a practical approach to them, or they can become an additional source of frustration.

Having a plan will help you organize your priorities. Preparations take time and energy. They are impossible to accomplish overnight. Having once made the decision as to what direction you will take, you are free to begin the necessary action to reach your specific goals.

If you have now become accustomed to making lists and gauging your progress by them, you may want to continue doing so. By writing out your goals, setting up your priorities, and placing them within suggested time frames, you will have a continuous record of your accomplishments. That should guarantee that the next time you are asked to describe yourself, you will have a ready list of positive characteristics to offer.

Worksheet: Working Out Your Plan

My decision is: _____

_____

My plan is: _____

_____

_____

_____

My goals are: Their time frames are:

1. _____   _____

   _____   _____

2. _____   _____

   _____   _____

3. _____   _____

   _____   _____

4. _____   _____

   _____   _____

5. _____   _____

   _____   _____

My priorities are:

1. _____

2. _____

3. _____

4. _____

5. _____

Turning Yourself Around

The last two chapters have been tools for checking your emotional pulse and for taking stock of your skills. They have pointed you in the direction you need to take, based on your decision. The next step is to make the preparations that will assure the attainment of your goal.

You will need to begin your preparation process by considering your emotions, just as you did in your self-assessment. Unless you are on firm ground and in control of how your decision will affect you, the rest of your preparations are likely to be slowed. Feeling emotionally strong and positive about your decision will add to your ability to move forward with confidence. It will also add to your ability to organize your preparations and to stay within the time limits you have designated. Being able to put the emotional trouble spots into a healthy perspective will ultimately conserve energy for you. This energy can then be turned toward concentrating on meeting the challenges that will result from your decision.

Return to your lists. Look at the elements listed for fear, anxiety, anger, and lack of self-confidence. Any of these that continue to have a major effect on your thought process or actions can become a serious block, even a disability. As we have already discussed, all of these emotions are normal. Under most circumstances they are to be expected. But it is necessary to work through them so that you control them. If you cannot, they are sure to hinder you and limit your progress. Beyond the self-help books and the assistance of friends, it may become advisable to seek professional counseling.

Along with your lists, you have already identified your weaknesses and your strengths. Following your arrival at a decision, you may want to revise them once again. They should provide you with some insights into how you can become mentally prepared for your planned changes. In this chapter we shall discuss some of the common trouble spots and make some suggestions for overcoming them.

Understanding

Change means leaving the familiar and facing the unknown. Understanding will be the axis, or turning point, from which we can once again tame the unfamiliar. Understanding is crucial to coping. The unknown becomes less threatening when we can fully comprehend the meaning of what is taking place or when we find acceptance, meaning, and significance in what we are doing.

When we experience something totally new or very different from any previous experience we have had, it is quite natural for us to assume that it is unique to us. This is rarely the case. Though the circumstances may be unique, the ramifications—the emotions created by the experience—are probably the same as others have also experienced. This fact is heavily endorsed by the increasing numbers of self-help and support groups being generated around many forms of illnesses and other life situations such as divorce, single parenting, and death of a spouse. What these groups offer is the sharing of common feelings and insights stemming from a relatively similar experience. It is not abnormal to feel isolated by the feelings generated from an unpleasant and frightening experience, but a sure way to dispel those feelings is to talk with others about them. Seek out those who have gone through similar events in their lives.

You have already spent time and effort discovering your fears and anxieties. Some will be specific to you and others will be shared by many. Fear of failure is certainly something many people experience. Even the most successful people have feelings of failure, rejection, and self-doubt. It is quite different, however, to recognize those feelings and to cope with them than to let them take charge of you. Begin by accepting that in any new venture fears are likely to exist. Failure is not on your agenda, though, and you do not need to set yourself up in a self-fulfilling prophecy. Eliminate those fears and anxieties that obviously have no factual basis. Then look at how you can translate the rest of your anxieties from negative factors to positive conditions. How many of them can be used to serve as reminders to be a bit more careful or cautious, a little more thoughtful or prepared before you take action on your plan? Use them as a safety net, but don't allow them to become stumbling blocks.

Anger can also be self-defeating. If you have already identified your anger, its source, and at what or whom you have directed it, you have taken some very important steps and are headed in the right direction. It may not be possible for you to completely resolve some areas of your anger or to let all of it go. That takes time, forgiveness, and patience. That does not mean that you must stay stuck in it either. Use it. Use it to your advantage and not against yourself. Many psychologists believe depression is anger turned inward at ourselves. Think about who benefits from dealing with your anger in that way. Certainly not you. On the other hand, the course of history has been changed by some very angry individuals who didn't agree with the way things were and decided there would be changes. Anger, properly channeled, can be a significant tool and stimulator of change. Take a touch of healthy fear of failing plus a dash of anger that says you'll get through this in spite of difficulties, and you come out with a strong set of motivations.

Raising Confidence Levels

Somewhere along the process of list making, you have become more in touch with how you see yourself. More likely than not you have made some discoveries that please you and some that do not. Remember now, we are attempting to translate those negative feelings into positive ones. Don't be too hard on yourself, but do be honest in your appraisal of which characteristics make you most unhappy.

These are the ones that will continue to be troublesome. Each time you make a step forward, the little nagging doubts will gnaw away the feelings of accomplishment. Perhaps that is why we often hear people say they feel as if they are moving two steps forward and three backward. To eliminate this source of frustration to the best of your ability, it is important to deal with the unsatisfactory aspects of your self-image.

Improving body image

Let's look at body image as an example. None of us is probably ever truly happy with ourselves. Some of us have lived as brunettes and always wondered if blonds really do have more fun—but not enough to make us want to change our hair color. Yet it is possible to do so. Weight is never right for most of us and is a constant battle. But if you really feel your weight is a handicap that will hold you back, do something about it. Diet books fill the shelves of bookstores and supermarkets. Weight clinics and exercise classes abound. Motivation is the most important ingredient in any diet or plan. If all your plans are going to fall apart because you are overweight, either you are not committed to your decision for change or you are motivated to do whatever is necessary to see your goals are met. No one ever said change would be easy.

Weight may not be the problem—or at least not the most immediate problem as you see it. Sometimes people experience a more general dissatisfaction. There aren't any magical solutions. Some things you really cannot change. For instance, you cannot change your height. But something any of us can do is make a few slight changes and try a little experimenting. A different haircut might make you feel as if you look taller, make your face look slimmer. Women who have worked at home for a number of years may have used the same style of makeup one season or year after another. It's easy to find out what the new trends are and fairly inexpensive to experiment a bit. Any new look, if you are pleased with it, can give you a lift. Clothing is another item that adds to self-esteem. It isn't always possible, but if you can, splurging on even a new blouse or shirt or putting together an outfit that will make you feel just right can give you a tremendous boost before you face an interview. Little changes or adjustments to your outer self can have a transforming effect. There is no question that looking good in your own eyes is a powerful confidence builder.

Emphasizing the positive

Self-image is not just body image. They overlap but are not one and the same, though they are sometimes mistaken for one another. How we see ourselves is more than what we glance at as we pass by a mirror. Our self-confidence is equally affected by what we think we are capable of. We generally do use our self-image as our measuring stick. What are you capable of? Look at your list of positive characteristics. Use feedback from friends. If they accept you as nurturing, helpful, and dependable, these are qualities you obviously display to others whether you feel you have them or not. Surely what they see in you must be justified. Chances are they are correct impressions and are indeed characteristics which you want to acknowledge and build on. They are assets to your self-image.

Gaining information

If you are insecure about your abilities for the career you have chosen, you may be bolstered by gaining more information about what is going on in that particular field. The simple remedy is to learn more. Investigate through books, trade journals, and specific magazine articles. Vocational counseling may also be helpful, although it will probably be more useful before you make your decision than after. The more you know about the particular position you are seeking, the more comfortable you will feel. The more comfortable you feel, the more confident you will be.

Once you feel as if you have a fairly clear view of what you will be getting into and what will be expected of you from your career choice, you can move on in your preparations. Seeking professional help with your résumé may also be a rewarding experience and a way to have someone else look at your credentials and qualifications. There will be more on the preparation of a résumé in a later chapter.

Taking risks

Now let us return to basics and discuss how confident you feel about your chances for completing this transition and gaining what you have set out as your goal. Scared? Of course you are. Most of us feel much safer if we can continue doing what we know we can do well. Now you are about to start all over without benefit of practice—but you can practice. What we are talking about is risk taking, something most of us would prefer not to do and seem to avoid if at all possible. Risk taking is what we can and really should practice. That involves decision making too. You have already made a big decision, but you can still practice on making small ones. Think of it as an exercise to tone the mind and condition your self-confidence.

To begin, think of something you have always wanted to do but have decided not to follow through on. Don't make it a big risk but one that could result in an enjoyable experience. It can be as simple as calling a friend you have had no contact with for years. The risk is that the person may not recognize your voice or even wish to talk with you. But what have you to lose? Make the decision to do it, follow up with action, and take the risk. Then repeat the process again with something that requires another small risk. One woman decided that risk taking was an important part of her growth and personal development. She made a resolution to take one risk per month. She started small; by the end of the year, she had increased her confidence level to the point where she decided to sign up for a survival course in winter camping.

Practicing people skills

Another area that often negates our self-confidence is our "people skills." We do not feel comfortable in meeting strangers. As a matter of fact, when placed in that situation, we feel downright awkward. If this is true for you, then set yourself up to practice these skills too. Force yourself to go out to meet new people in new environments. If you begin away from your familiar surroundings, you will have less invested. For instance, what difference will it make to your life if you strike out in a conversation you start with a store clerk? How about someone sitting next to you in a restaurant? Parties and meetings are good places to practice social skills with new people, and yet many times we tend to ignore new people in favor of those we already know. Be friendly and speak to someone on an elevator. That's all that it takes, but the habit will become more natural to you. Combine risk taking and social skills and speak out at a meeting of some group. Afterward see if your self-image has changed, your confidence level has been raised somewhat. You may just find yourself feeling pretty good about your progress.

Being assertive

There is one more area that should be mentioned here, and that is assertiveness. Many people have trouble dealing with others who would take advantage of them. Often it seems more expedient to say yes than no. Men and women may have difficulty in expressing their ideas or stating their needs in ways that are nonthreatening to friends and co-workers. Fortunately, there are many self-help books and seminars available to teach the art of assertiveness. Learning and practicing these skills are not only interesting and fun, but they will add to your self-confidence level. Imagine how good you will feel about yourself when you are able to hold your ground with an aggressive salesperson or gain service from an unwilling repair provider.

Ego Involvement and Protection

Along with raising our self-confidence level, we are also feeding our ego. When we head in new directions, make changes, and take risks, we are involving ego as well as self. Consider the financial rewards of a career. Would the offer of a larger than expected salary mean more strokes for your ego? How about the length of time it takes for you to actually gain a position? Does your ego get more points if you are hired quickly than if the search goes on for months? It is necessary to acknowledge what is at stake in seeking a new career or reentering the work force. You need to be aware of what is being invested and to what degree in order to protect yourself and your ego.

As any of you who have job hunted in the past are well aware, rejection is part of it. For every job available, only one person will be hired. Each time you make an application, the same rule applies. The more jobs you apply for, the more chances there are that you will experience this form of rejection. Not being hired is disappointing, but it has nothing to do with your personal worth. Keep that in mind. As a matter of fact, dwell on that pertinent fact. Resolve to maintain a rational perspective on job attainment versus personal goal achievements. Repeated disappointments, which are common in job hunting, are wearing and discouraging. Accept them in the best way you can and continue to move on. It is easy to get bogged down and begin to feel sorry for yourself, but also self-defeating. This is not a test of your self-worth. Your ego will be bruised only if you allow it to be.

Mental Preparedness

Practicing positive thinking

Now is the time for positive thinking. In fact, there is a lot being written about its benefits. We have all known people who have had the odds stacked against them and yet have come through miraculously. Think of those who have re-covered from illnesses after all hope was given up or those who have had their homes destroyed or their families lost in disasters such as earthquakes, floods, and fires. Some-how they have found the will to go on, to pick up the pieces of their lives and to rebuild, to start again. If you have not read one of the numerous books on positive thinking, do so now. It will help you in becoming a believer in yourself.

It is assumed here that you have prepared yourself to take the practical steps that have been suggested in order to raise your self-confidence level. Along with experiencing the risk taking and becoming satisfied with your self im-age, you will discover that you do have abilities for coping and survival. Those of you who are making a reentry into the work force, and especially those of you who are doing so because of necessity, have at times probably questioned whether you would survive or not. You are not alone in this feeling. Many people have at some time reached a point where they did not think it possible to regain their lost ground. Some people feel as if they have fallen to the bottom of a deep hole and wish to start the climb out, only to find they have not reached the bottom yet. Do not de-spair. Change that direction by taking charge of your own destiny and working to change the situations that seem to surround you. That is positive thinking and believing in yourself and your abilities. Most of us really are survivors whether we have ever thought ourselves so or not. Once you recognize that, it will change your attitude about many things, especially how you see yourself.

Gathering information

In mentally preparing yourself to seek the job that will start your new career, do everything possible to feel as comfortable as you can. The more you know about the com-pany where you are applying, the more at ease you will be in writing a cover letter or doing an interview. Arm your-self with as much information as you can. Having a good résumé ready to send out will also make you feel more sure of yourself. Do whatever is necessary to stimulate your mo-tivation and get that start in the career of your choice.

Looking at the job-hunting process

Another way to mentally prepare yourself is to examine how you look at the job-hunting process. Actually it is an ongoing process that will continue in one form or another the rest of your career. Therefore, what you start with now is not what you will eventually end up with. Thinking in those terms leaves room for future development and change. Your first job is only the beginning. If you have decided to make a substantial career change, in all likelihood you will not be starting at the same level you left. Making a reentry after a long period of being out of the work force may mean you will need to begin below your potential ability in order to gain work experience and prove yourself. To begin you may have to settle for less than you had hoped for, but know that it is not a "forever" situation and be aware of what your chances are for upward mobility.

Helping Yourself

Understanding what is happening and why is the first step to putting positive thinking to good use. Next, you want to reach some level of self-acceptance. You won't accomplish this overnight, but that isn't necessary. Remember, it's a process, one of thinking, doing, and experiencing. Actually it's a process you've been in since the day of your birth. The difference now is that you have found a motivation for making a change. That change is focused on your career. Your energy will be directed toward that goal. Anything that will assist you in reaching it is specifically what you will want to include in this phase of your process.

What has been described in this chapter are small but significant steps you can take to help yourself. Most of them, such as learning to take risks, can be done quite easily and can be fun as well as rewarding. Feeling good about yourself and what you can accomplish—and have accomplished—is pleasurable. Once you start doing things that add to your good feeling and positive thinking, you may find yourself hooked and want to continue.

Keep track of your positive progress. Listen to those compliments that others offer you and sincerely accept them. As you develop your positive thinking and self-image, you may note a change in others' responses to you. Self-confidence can be contagious. What your family and friends once took for granted in you, they may now have to reexamine. Hopefully the supportive people around you will not be adverse to giving you good feedback about your changes. And certainly we all know how much better others feel about being around us when we are in an upbeat frame of mind.

You can add to this if you give yourself some positive strokes too. Each time you feel you have handled a difficult or new and unusual situation quite well, allow yourself to take well-earned pride in your accomplishment. Consider how you might have dealt with the predicament in the past before the "new you" emerged. And don't forget to see some humor in it all. Confident people can laugh at themselves as well as with others.

There is just one word of caution, and it fits with your understanding and need for acceptance. Please realize that not every day will bring significant progress. Some days you just won't feel as good about yourself as others. No one's energy is at the same level day after day. Some days you will need to put yourself on hold and simply mark time. You must be prepared, too, to be tolerant of those days when you actually feel as if you have moved backward. Backsliding is also part of the process; if you are willing to accept it as such, it will not become a stumbling block but will just be a part of the ebb and flow of the entire movement. Don't be your own worst enemy by letting negative feelings berate you. Instead, wait for this period to pass, as pass it will, and continue to set those mini-objectives for your continued accomplishments.

Worksheet: Turning Yourself Around

Place a check mark in front of the items that might help you in your preparations for attaining your goal.

_____ join a support group where you can share your feelings with others who have had similar experiences

_____ analyze your fears and turn them into positive conditions

_____ identify your anger and use it to your advantage

_____ make body image improvements

_____ gain information about the career you have chosen

One way to raise your confidence level is to practice taking small risks, such as calling a friend you haven't spoken to in years or striking up a conversation with a stranger. List five small risks you will take during the next month and record the outcomes:

Small risk 1: _____

Outcome: _____

_____

_____

_____

Small risk 2: _____

Outcome: _____

Small risk 3: _____

Outcome: _____

Small risk 4: _____

Outcome: _____

_____

_____

_____

_____

Small risk 5: _____

Outcome: _____

_____

_____

_____

_____

List three steps you will take toward improving your assertiveness:

1. _____

_____

_____

2. _____

_____

_____

3. _____

_____

_____

Preparation and Follow Through

This book discusses a process, one oriented to your career. It begins with your recognizing a need for change. The process then moves on to a phase of decision making and finally the stage of preparation. This last stage can be the most time consuming, depending on what preparations will be required of you.

Until this final stage, there appears to be less need to differentiate between those who are making a reentry into the work force and those who have decided to make a career change to upgrade their present position. However, those forced into the decision-making process by crisis probably will have more emotional aspects to cope with than those who are able to come to this decision for change by choice. Otherwise, change is change, and it is, at best, an unsettling experience for all of us.

The process appears to work the same for people making this change in both categories. However, it would be unfair not to acknowledge that in the phase of preparation there may be some distinct differences between the two groups. If you have been continually involved in the work force, you will more likely understand the ground rules of employment. You may already be fully aware of the politics involved. Unless you are making a significant or diverse change in careers, you may also be fairly current with what is going on in your specific choice of industry. For those of you making reentry into the work force after years of absence, these areas could place you at a disadvantage. In this chapter we shall attempt to sharpen your awareness skills and help you relearn the "game".

Credentials If you need them, get them. Sometimes there is no way around this. Credentials may be educational or legal requirements. Many careers require licenses or certification as well as completion of an educational process. From your previous research, you will have learned what is required and expected from your chosen area. Licenses and board certifications are regulated by law. If these are part of the career you have chosen, you must meet requirements, because no employer can accept you without proof of such. The regulations and procedure may vary from state to state, so you will need to know exactly what will be necessary for you.

Education credentials are often set standards that are accepted by most employers. Some employers may be willing to substitute one form of education for another, including experience. However, this is not always possible depending on company rules and what regulations or accreditation standards must be met.

Many careers have various levels of entry and a possibility of advancing from one level to another as more education is gained. One example is nursing. It is possible to enter this health career by meeting minimal requirements. Through a vocational program, one may be certified as a nursing assistant. While working at that level, it is possible to attend more classes in order to complete a practical nurse program. Following licensure as a licensed practical nurse, one can continue both working and going to classes for a diploma or baccalaureate degree in nursing, thereby becoming prepared for licensure as a registered nurse. It is possible to obtain a master's or doctorate degree in nursing as well. Other careers, such as psychology and social work, offer baccalaureate degrees as do many science specialties, but career opportunities are severely limited until the master's level is obtained.

Know what you need. Know where you can start. Have a plan.

Job Search   Quite obviously, before you can apply for a job, you must first locate one that is available. The types of resources, such as newspaper ads and employment agencies, will be covered in detail in a later chapter of this book. Hopefully what you have been doing (since before your decision-making process was complete) was to have tuned into some of these resources so that you will have a fair idea of what is being offered. Newspaper and magazine advertisements might even give you a clue as to what salaries and benefits are offered by various employers for the level of job for which you wish to apply. This can be particularly helpful for those of you making a reentry, as things may have changed a great deal since you last took notice. It is important for you to have some idea of whether an offer made to you is fair, high, or low. Many ads will also include expected qualifications. Again, this is helpful information.

Adopt a bold and creative attitude. Where do you want to work, for whom, doing what? If you know these things, you can go to that source and check it out, even make an application. You may be told there is nothing open at this time, but you should ask that your application and résumé be kept on file. In many types of employment, there are ways to get in on the ground floor. If this would work for you, figure out a way to do it. People have been known to volunteer their time just to get in the door. Once in, you will not only be able to prove your value to the group, but you will be around to know when something does become available.

The one very valuable asset people who are already in the work force have over those who are not is contacts. We have all heard the saying "it is not what you know, but who you know." There is a great deal of truth to that statement. Each business has its own networking system. If you are fortunate enough to have someone from within that system who is willing to be of help to you, by all means graciously accept his or her offer. If you are not so lucky, then think of what other contacts you may have. Many people relied heavily on their contacts while going through job changes in the past and planned to use those resources again. One person kept a record over the years of people, business and personal acquaintances, whom she might consider as resources or who could at least further her contact system. All this may sound cold and calculating, but actually it is not. It is good business that is done every day. It is all part of the "game."

You may be surprised to find how small the world can be. People you may never have expected may be able to assist you. One person was offered a job by his landlord. Another was requested to make an application by her future employer because he had heard of the fine job she was doing for her then present employer. It happens. Not everyone will step forward on their own. If you are making a career change or reentry, it is perfectly logical to seek out someone in that field for some expert advice. Most people are flattered by being placed in that position, and their suggestions may also include possible job openings.

A word of caution. You will, of course, want to use good judgment in this matter. It is not being suggested that all acquaintances are good contacts, nor are all contacts good resources. Then, too, if you are presently employed and do not wish to have your employer know that you are planning a change, some discretion will be necessary in utilizing contacts. There will be more on contacts and networking in the following chapter also.

Marketing Yourself

Most of us have difficulty marketing ourselves. We are not accustomed to thinking about ourselves in these terms. Yet we are more practiced than we realize. Every time we meet someone new, have an idea we wish others to accept, or have a request of someone, we are presenting ourselves in the most advantageous way we can. "Best foot forward" is the old adage. That is what marketing yourself for the job is all about too.

If you have followed through with the lists it was suggested you make, then you already have identified your positive assets and characteristics. Those are the ones you want woven into your résumé, and those are the ones you want an opportunity to talk about in an interview. There is nothing wrong with promoting our own good qualities, even though we may have been taught differently as children. We are no longer children, though we sometimes feel like it when we begin new experiences. We are also capable of distinguishing between a braggart and someone who believes in herself or himself. So can a future employer. Taking a sincere approach toward the advancement of your own cause is unreproachable behavior. Graciously accepting credit for a job well done is admirable. It is also part of self-confidence. This is a serious matter. There is competition out there, and lest you forget, only one person will get the job.

There is no rule that says you cannot apply for a job that interests you even though you do not meet all the qualifications requested. Chances are the employer—while looking for the ideal person to fill the position—does not realistically expect to find such a person. The employer may be interested in accepting some of your qualifications as viable tradeoffs or substitutions. You will never know unless you make the application. It is the risk you have been practicing for. And once more remind yourself that if it does not work out, it is not a personal rejection.

You may also learn of a job opening for which you are certain you are qualified. The job sounds like something you would really like to try. You feel certain you could easily do the work. This often happens for those persons making reentry as well as career changes. The prospective job may not be extremely challenging, but it offers you a comfort zone to begin in. You march in very confidently only to be turned down for the job because you are told you are overqualified. The employer does not believe you would be happy in that position. One such woman expressed how extremely frustrating and discouraging this situation was for her. Because she did not have the educational credentials to start at a level above the one she applied for, she felt this was where she must begin. But the common answer was that she was overqualified. The woman finally coaxed an employer into giving her a try at the position by saying she would be happy to accept additional responsibilities not listed in the current job description.

Marketing yourself and your talents will be easier if you keep in mind the growth you have experienced just within this process. From the start you must have felt there was something better out there waiting for you. What you have done for yourself—and mostly by yourself—has brought you this far. Take pride in those accomplishments and share them now with the outside world.

Assertiveness

This skill, as we have suggested before, can be of great help to you. The term assertiveness sometimes carries a negative connotation or receives an emotionally laden response. This is really unfair. Asssertiveness is a respectable trait. It is neither manipulative nor aggressive. It is a tool, a social plus as well as a business and career asset. Learning to express yourself in a positive, nonthreatening way is a valuable communication tool. Assertiveness helps us to accept our humanness and also sets realistic limits to what we can expect of ourselves and of others. These skills can help us feel more comfortable with rejection and criticism, both of which we will encounter in the work world.

In practicing assertiveness, we are given permission to say "I don't know" and "I don't understand" without feeling inadequate. It allows us to ask questions. Assertiveness opens two-way communications. Do not apologize for or defend the use of assertiveness. Learn it and enjoy the practice of it.

Check Out Your Prospects

Learning about employers

Several times in earlier chapters it has been suggested that you learn more about your prospective employer. Sources such as professional journals, newspapers, and magazine articles have been mentioned. In some instances, these will yield nothing. If you are checking on a small operation, phone calls to the place itself will be unproductive and could be misconstrued. Asking around within the community and relying on word-of-mouth reports may be misleading. If you run into these kinds of blank walls, it is probably better just to go in with an open mind and ask questions there.

Each company has its own application policy, as you will learn in more detail in the upcoming chapters. Briefly though, some will request you make an application in person while others will request you send a résumé. When making an application in person, you may have contact only with a receptionist or perhaps a person from the personnel department. Rarely will you meet the person actually responsible for the hiring of a specific position on your first call. A person from personnel, however, may have access to a job description and benefits assigned to the open position. One can at least ask. Whoever is responsible for taking the application from you should be informed as to the employer's hiring practice. That person most likely can tell you when the position is expected to be filled and how you will be notified of an interview. Do not hesitate to inquire. It shows you're interested.

Managing the interview

Whether or not you have been able to check out your prospective employer, have some questions ready for your interview. Asking questions makes you an active participant, not just a respondent. If you are an effective listener, you will be able to fit your questions into the general design or pattern of the interview, and they will be appropriate questions.

Effective listening during an interview will intensify your concentration and reduce your nervousness. You'll be too busy listening to worry about inconsequential things. It may also give you clues as to what your employer is looking for in regard to qualifications and personality traits. After all, the name of the game is to be able to give the answers the employer wants to hear.

Understanding the system

Next, we shall assume you have been hired to fill a position. Congratulations! But the preparation is still not complete, nor has your investigation ended. For those of you who are making a reentry, this may come as a shock to you, but you have just joined a political group. This group concentrates not on elections but on promotions.

There is not a group made up of two or more persons working for the same organization that will not have its political overtones and undertows. It would be naive to think otherwise. Again, effective listening and appropriate questioning are your tools for unlocking the mysteries. Identify your group's power bases, formal and informal. Who makes the big decisions, the little decisions? Who is the leader by power of authority, by virtue of personality? Understand the chain of command, the corporate structure, and whether it is effective or not. Be alert to the management style. Is it authoritative, directive, or democratic? Does one person establish objectives and make the decision as to how and by whom they will be carried out? This is an authoritative style. Does the group become involved with the process at least to the point of being able to give feedback and opinions, even though the final decision will still be made by the person in charge of the group? This is a directive style. Or does the group itself, as a whole body, sit down with its leader to make the decisions in a thoroughly democratic way? This is, of course, a democratic style.

It takes time and effort to get to know your employer's systems, but understanding them will be as useful to your success as getting to understand yourself has been.

A large part of any preparation is mental preparedness, being aware of and ready to respond to the possibilities we are about to face. Rarely can we be totally prepared for all the unexpected events that might occur. But if we know the rules of the "game," we can use them as guidelines. That is all that is being suggested. Be aware of the possibilities, understand the basics.

In this chapter, we have jumped ahead and placed you in a job setting only to make the point that there are rules within the system as well as rules that apply to getting into the system. You will take many of the skills you have developed through this process to your new career. The practice and development of your skills will continue. You will find them applicable in numerous areas of your life. Self-confidence, risk taking, decision making, and assertiveness will serve you well. You may even find that list making becomes a habit for clarifying goals and objectives outside your career as well as in your job performance.

Your coping skills have been tested in this process of change. They will continue to be tested and stretched. You are becoming more resilient and flexible. Because it deserves the repetition we are giving it, we repeat, this process of change is ongoing and unceasing. Each time you are faced with another major decision, you will need to begin the process at the beginning. But the next decision, and those that follow, will find you are more practiced and more willing to move from one stage to the next. You will do so with less stress than you experienced the first time.

The mental and emotional phases that have been described thus far are the ones that have been identified in men and women who have gone through this process. The stages you will go through may not be identical to the ones documented here. You will be on safe ground as long as you are aware of the importance of being unencumbered by major emotional battles before you reach the point of making a decision. Making a decision from strength and understanding will give you a better chance of fulfilling your goals. The stage of preparation is part of the transition you make from the past to your future endeavors. There is more to follow on the practical side of those preparations.

Worksheet: Record of My Job Search

You may want to photocopy this worksheet before you fill it in so that you will have more space for future job search records.

Resources/Contacts

Name of contact: _____

Date of conversation: _____

Outcome: _____

Name of contact: _____

Date of conversation: _____

Outcome: _____

Name of contact: _____

Date of conversation: _____

Outcome: _____

Name of contact: _____

Date of conversation: _____

Outcome: _____

Name of contact: _____

Date of conversation: _____

Outcome: _____

Résumés

Résumé sent to: _____

Date sent: _____

Outcome: _____

Résumé sent to: _____

Date sent: _____

Outcome: _____

Résumé sent to: _____

Date sent: _____

Outcome: _____

Résumé sent to: _____

Date sent: _____

Outcome: _____

Résumé sent to: _____

Date sent: _____

Outcome: _____

Résumé sent to: _____

Date sent: _____

Outcome: _____

Interviews

Interviewed with: _____

Date of interview: _____

Impressions and outcome: _____

_____

Interviewed with: _____

Date of interview: _____

Impressions and outcome: _____

_____

Interviewed with: _____

Date of interview: _____

Impressions and outcome: _____

_____

Interviewed with: _____

Date of interview: _____

Impressions and outcome: _____

_____

Interviewed with: _____

Date of interview: _____

Impressions and outcome: _____

_____

Starting the Job Search

We have devoted considerable time showing how those of you planning a new career are surrounded by a different set of circumstances from those just starting the search for their first job or looking for the next step in their career progression. We cannot overemphasize the fact that you are making a very significant change. You are not functioning within the comfortable cocoon of going up the ladder. You are breaking out into unknown territories and changing your life patterns. The more you can use the past in shaping and making the future, the greater your chances for success.

In earlier chapters we have suggested that you make several lists—fears, anxieties, positives and negatives, and a history of your experiences and accomplishments. You have used these lists in preparing yourself for change. They have helped you to identify the direction in which to concentrate your efforts. Don't throw them away. You are now going to use those lists extensively as you become involved in the mechanics of finding a job.

How to Find the Jobs   There have been instances when jobs were created for a particular person after an interview. However, such occasions are rare, particularly at the level where most reentries and career changers start. Most of you will be looking for positions already in existence, jobs newly created because of expansion, or new business start-ups. Information about these jobs can be obtained by using any of four basic job search methods:

1. advertising

2. governmental or private sector agencies

3. networking

4. shotgunning

Advertising   The classified ad in newspaper and trade publications is the most visible and often-used job search method. It is estimated that from 10 percent to 25 percent of jobs are actually filled through classified ads. For some, it is the only game in town, and they rely completely on the newspaper for job information. Using classified ads for job information should not be discouraged, but you should know a few facts about them.

Classified ads are the most competitive. It is not usual for a newspaper ad to draw two hundred or more inquiries or résumés, and sometimes as many as five hundred. Unfortunately, the sheer numbers often mean that most responses are not even read. The employer will pick the five people to be interviewed out of the first fifty responses received. Otherwise, the time necessary to process all the résumés would slow down the interviewing process considerably. In cases involving governmental agencies or companies with considerable government contracts, all the résumés and applications must be processed according to a strict procedure. Thus, filling the position can take months.

Some of the ads are for positions already filled. Placing the ad was a matter of contract, policy, or law. As the vacancy occurred, someone already employed at the company was identified as the most likely candidate having all the necessary qualifications and the experience. However, because of affirmative action requirements and company or agency policy, the organization went through the motions of recruiting publicly for the position.

Some ads are deliberately misleading. By using such phrases as *leading to management positions, potential income in the high sixties,* and *high visibility and income,* some companies recruit for commission-only positions selling products and services that can only be considered as highly questionable. Others may use these terms in a completely legitimate manner, recruiting to fill positions with the stated potentials.

Some ads will give instructions for the procedure to be used to apply for the position. They may read ''submit résumé,'' ''apply in person between 9 and 4,'' ''call between 9 and 4,'' or ''send résumé only, do not call.'' Generally, if you disregard the instructions, you will eliminate yourself from the competition, even though some books and articles advocate so-called creative ways of submitting applications to gain attention. Consider one fact before you become too creative. Many companies and organizations have established strict recruiting and hiring procedures because of affirmative action, OEO (Office of Equal Opportunity) requirements, contract stipulations, and other efforts to reduce exposure to litigation or claims involving discriminatory hiring practices. To be considered, you must play the game their way.

If you use classified ads in newspaper or trade publications as a source of job leads, then do so in an organized and efficient manner. Keep records of the jobs for which you apply plus information from the ad or the follow-up. By maintaining these records, you can avoid duplicate applications. More important, these records will help you in deciding whether you should waste your time in following through. For example, if an ad that seems consistantly vague reappears almost every week, then a little warning light should go off alerting you that this position may be of questionable value. These records will also help you in identifying responses.

Here are some hints to follow when responding to classified ads.

Follow instructions   Follow instructions, particularly when responding to ads placed by government agencies, large companies, nonprofit educational institutions, and companies with large government contracts.

Time your response   Should you respond as soon as possible? This depends upon the source of the ad. Many ads will contain a closing date or a deadline. Usually, if an organization advertises a closing date, it will consider all applications meeting that deadline because it is part of its established procedure or policy. Government agencies and educational institutions will also have closing dates, even though they may not be advertised.

If the recruiting organization is in the private sector or you cannot tell who placed the ad, then act as soon as possible. One well-designed advertisement recruiting for several positions elicited seven thousand applications. Often recruiters are pressured to fill positions as soon as possible. They will set up interviews as soon as they find five or six promising candidates, sometimes within a day or two. If one of this first group of candidates is hired, none of the later applications is considered.

Screen all ads   When screening ads for positions that may interest you, screen the entire section, not just the part that you assume will contain your type of position. For example, if you are seeking something in advertising, do not assume that all the available positions will be listed under *A*. Some papers will print ads alphabetically according to the first letter of the first sentence. Consequently, ads that read, "Urgently needed, an advertising professional" or "Progressive salon needs experienced hairdresser" will be placed far from the *A*'s for advertising or the *H*'s for hairdressers. Other papers seem to use little reason or logic when printing ads, and your potential position could be advertised anywhere.

Furnish a résumé   Be prepared to furnish a résumé to those companies or organizations that request that you call or apply in person. Remember, the number of applications usually received means that is impossible for the organization to interview everyone. The critical decision as to who will be interviewed will still be based on your résumé.

Be prepared   When responding to an ad that provides a phone number to call, be prepared for almost anything. If the company is a large one, the person answering the phone will probably be a personnel clerk or a secretary whose primary responsibility will be one or more of the following:

- inform you that a résumé should be sent to a certain address

- inform you that applications can be picked up at a certain address or tell you that an application will be mailed to you

- inform you as to what information is preferred in a résumé

- provide you with basic information and qualifications required and then ask for a résumé if you are still interested.

- conduct a preliminary interview and inform you as to whether or not you should continue by asking for a résumé or setting up another interview

In a small company, the person answering the phone could be a key person in the personnel department, the secretary to the person doing the hiring (potentially critical to being hired), or the actual person doing the hiring. The impression created by the first contact, even though it is by phone, is extremely important.

Be prepared for talking with the person doing the actual hiring, and anyone less than that person can be handled with confidence. Writing out your questions ahead of time, making notes about your qualifications, and even doing a little rehearsing will enable you to handle any situation with confidence.

Regardless of the method required for the initial contact—phone call, résumé, application, or actual visit—your principal objective is to obtain that first interview. Your response to the ad, therefore, should be carefully thought out and prepared. Your phone conversation, the cover letter for the résumé or application, and the impression you create during an office visit are your opportunities to gain an edge over the other applicants. If you are not willing to give your best effort at this stage of the process, then don't bother to answer the ad.

Worksheet: Responding to an Ad

Write down the following information about every ad that you respond to during the course of your job search. Whenever possible attach the ad or other information about the job obtained from the print media. You may want to photocopy this worksheet before filling it in so you will have more space for future records.

Job title: _____

Date of ad: _____

Source: _____

Requested qualifications and job description: _____

_____

_____

Response address: _____

_____

Name of addressee: _____ Phone: _____

Type of response: _____ résumé _____ phone _____ visit

Date of response: _____ follow-up dates: _____

Result: _____

_____

_____

Job title: _____

Date of ad: _____

Source: _____

Requested qualifications and job description: _____

_____

_____

Response address: _____

_____

Name of addressee: _____ Phone: _____

Type of response: _____ résumé _____ phone _____ visit

Date of response: _____ follow-up dates: _____

Result: _____

_____

_____

Job title: _____

Date of ad: _____

Source: _____

Requested qualifications and job description: _____

_____

_____

Response address: _____

_____

Name of addressee: _____ Phone: _____

Type of response: _____ résumé _____ phone _____ visit

Date of response: _____ follow-up dates: _____

Result: _____

_____

_____

Employment Agencies and Offices

At one time or another, almost everyone who has searched for employment has contacted some type of an employment agency in either the government or the private sector. Unfortunately, there are numerous types of employment agencies, some highly respected and productive and some very expensive and useless. In general, agencies and offices can be classified as follows.

State employment agencies

Generally you can find state employment agencies in almost all urban centers. There is no fee involved since they are subsidized by the federal government. The state agency will list predominantly unskilled and semiskilled positions, although occasionally higher paid technical, professional, or managerial jobs are posted. The state employment office may be of use to those of you who wish to get your foot in the door with the hopes of being promoted rapidly.

Private employment agencies

Private employment agencies are divided into several subgroups based on the types of positions offered, the methods of charging fees, and whether the employment services are for permanent positions or temporary services. Many agencies specialize in certain types of employment, such as accounting, bookkeeping, engineering, clerical or computer. Others specialize in the executive and managerial levels. Some agencies specialize in fee-paid positions—the employer pays the search fee if they find you a position that you accept. Some offer only employment services for which you pay the fees if you accept the position, and others will offer both arrangements. In some cases, payment of the fee is a negotiable item similar to salary and fringe benefits.

Obviously, reading the contract and understanding it is of critical importance with private agencies. Make sure that you understand who pays the fees and under what circumstances. For example, find out who pays if you take a position and then leave in three months or if you are terminated from a position after two months.

Many private employment agencies are franchise operations. Although there may be branches throughout the country, there is no guarantee that your résumé will be circulated among the other franchises unless it is stated in the contract.

Employment consulting agencies

There are agencies advertising in the paper constantly that are not actually employment agencies. They do not list available jobs nor do they attempt to negotiate or find a job for you. Their primary function is to teach you how to find a job—résumé preparation, personal grooming, interview techniques—and some will bombard companies on a nationwide basis with your résumés. The fees are substantial, usually $2,500 to $5,000, and the results vary.

Executive search agencies (headhunters)

Most headhunters are employed by companies on a fee basis to find specific types of employees for executive positions. They usually look among the ranks of those already employed and induce them to change companies. Some will take résumés, but don't hold your breath waiting for action.

Company personnel offices

Most larger companies have personnel offices that accept applications and résumés on a continuing basis. However, using these offices is usually only effective when you are seeking a job at the semiskilled or unskilled level, where there is a continuous turnover and need. Occasionally you may hit them just when they need someone of your qualifications, but the odds are not very good. You may ask them to keep your résumé on file, but this type of application is active for only two or three weeks at best.

Networking

The term networking refers to the use of contacts, acquaintances, relatives, former co-workers, or other person-to-person sources of information to obtain knowledge about existing possibilities for employment. A network is a system of lines or channels (of communication) that interlace like the fabric of a net. If you use the networking approach, you will open as many channels of communication as you can to find out who is hiring.

Perhaps the majority of jobs are found using the network approach. A relative or a friend will mention the fact that a certain company is looking for employees, the word is passed through a trade association that a certain position will be open, a friend mentions you to an employer for a certain position. In fact, companies are using networking when they pass the word among their employees that they are looking to fill existing positions or to expand. Employers are increasingly using their own employees as recruiters because it is an economical and highly efficient way to find new employees. Generally employees are reluctant to recommend anyone in whom they are not confident because the new employee's action will reflect on their own judgment.

Networking is not limited only to those people you know. Often you can get information about positions from people who are familiar with an industry or a company. For example, the executive director of a trade association is often familiar with all of the members of the association and is frequently aware of pending openings; salespersons often know of openings in client companies. In many cases, your contact may wish to remain anonymous. Such requests should be honored; you may need that person's information again sometime.

You should also be aware that there are organizations in which networking is a basic goal. Many cities have organizations specifically organized to help women find positions. Professional or trade organizations are also excellent sources of information.

Do not be reluctant to put out the word that you want to change careers or reenter the workplace. Remember that most of the people you contact have used the same method themselves and will be sympathetic and helpful. Perhaps you feel awkward about admitting that you are looking for another job, but if you do not use the network approach, you are avoiding the most productive method of finding employment.

Shotgunning

The term shotgunning is just what it sounds like: firing off many résumés to various companies or organizations and hoping that you can stir up some interest. Shotgunning is the most expensive and usually the least productive of all the methods of finding a job. Even so, many employment agencies and counselors use this approach. Many people who have used this approach, usually at the managerial level, have not had very satisfying experiences. Most report that they receive only one or two acknowledgments—whether negative or positive—from every hundred résumés mailed. One reported eight responses and two interviews out of seven hundred résumés mailed.

Blame the computer for one reason companies are not very responsive to shotgun résumés. One personnel manager reported that he receives scores of résumés each day from employment agencies or counselors who have sold the concept of blanketing the industry with résumés to their clients. These unsolicited résumés are handled like junk mail—screened out and discarded.

As a career changer or one reentering the job market, you should use at least some of the elements of all four of the basic methods outlined in this chapter, because if you do not know about a job opening, you can't apply for it. Once you have readied and committed yourself to finding a job, the more jobs you consider, the better your chances of finding the right one.

As a career changer or a reenterer, your search for a job is complicated by the lack of recent or relevant experience, and you will probably find that it is somewhat difficult to obtain that first interview. Under these circumstances, networking will probably stand the greatest chance of being productive. If you can find someone willing to introduce you to a prospective employer or to recommend you, then your chances of success are far greater than by answering ads or making cold calls.

Again, your situation is a complicated one, much more complex than the so-called "normal" job search. Because of the complexity, you will have some frustrating, even maddening, experiences. Keep one important fact in mind. These experiences are the result of your situation, not your lack of worth or ability; it will require patience, confidence, and perseverance to find the job you want.

Worksheet: Planning Your Job Search

List the types of jobs that interest you:

1. _____
2. _____
3. _____
4. _____
5. _____

List the newspapers and other publications that carry advertisements concerning these positions.

1. _____
2. _____
3. _____
4. _____

List the major companies or organizations that normally hire people for the type of position you are looking for.

1. _____
2. _____
3. _____
4. _____
5. _____

Identify the people that you know or know of within these companies or organizations.

1. Name _____   Organization _____
2. Name _____   Organization _____
3. Name _____   Organization _____
4. Name _____   Organization _____
5. Name _____   Organization _____

List possible information sources (trade associations, customers, clients, personnel departments)

1. _____
2. _____
3. _____
4. _____

How Employers Use Résumés

As you look through the classified ads for employment, you will notice that many ask you to send a résumé. Even when you call in response to an ad listing a telephone number, in most cases, a résumé will be requested. Applications for positions ranging from entry level to president of the company include requirements for résumés. Requiring résumés for such a broad range of positions is a relatively new idea. Twenty to thirty years ago, résumés were usually required only for high-level executive, professional, academic, and highly technical positions. Consequently, many of you currently employed have never prepared one. Now résumés are a common requirement and are certainly a must in any job search.

Before you begin to prepare your résumé, you must understand precisely what a résumé is and, most important, how it is processed and used by the organization seeking to fill a position. How the résumé is processed critically affects the design, format, and content of your résumé for reasons explained later in this chapter. At this point, however, we shall define the purpose of the résumé.

The Purpose of the Résumé

The résumé is an application for a position. Granted, there are occasions when a résumé might be used in conjunction with a business loan application or an appointment to a governing board, but these instances are comparatively rare. The use of the résumé as an application may be for a specific position or for an unspecified position in a general career field. It describes your background in terms of employment experience, education, and training; it also includes other information that may be relevant to the position for which you are applying. It can also describe special accomplishments, honors, or projects that are relevant.

Why Employers Require a Résumé

Several decades ago, the résumé was used only as a guide to an interviewer. Currently, the résumé is often your only chance to get that first interview. But remember this: the résumé can get you the interview, not the job. It is probably the only device that you have to advertise or market yourself. Far too many people dash off something in response to an ad and say to themselves, "I'll be able to tell them how qualified I am and how good an employee I'll be during the interview." The days when all applicants are interviewed are gone forever. If you understand that an employer who receives five hundred résumés for one opening will usually interview only four to eight people, then you begin to understand how important that résumé can be.

There are numerous sources of advice on how to prepare a résumé. High school and college counselors, employment counselors, and résumé writers are just a few of the sources. There are also numerous books written on the subject that offer valuable advice. However, few of these sources pay sufficient attention to what happens to that résumé after it is delivered to the potential employer. Few explain how the processing of a résumé by the employer can determine how the résumé should be formatted.

There are several key factors about the organization to which you wish to apply that you must consider before you design your résumé. Consider these questions:

■ What type of organization is it? Private business, governmental, public educational, or private business involved in many government contracts?

■ What is the size of the organization? Does it operate out of several locations, and is the hiring centralized or decentralized?

■ Who first receives the résumé: a general receptionist, a personnel clerk, or the secretary for the person actually making the final decision?

■ How many résumés are usually received for an advertised position?

■ Who is responsible for doing the initial screening of the résumé?

■ Who is responsible for the initial evaluation of the résumé?

■ Is the organization in question subject to strict affirmative action and equal opportunity employment regulations?

■ Is there a separate personnel department?

The answers to many of these questions are a matter of common sense if you know who has placed the ad or if you are familiar with the company. In situations involving blind ads (box numbers only), you can only make assumptions based on the ad's size and content. For example, small companies seldom take out expensive block ads. Unusual phrasing or incomplete information are usually indicative of smaller organizations without much recruiting experience.

If you know the source of the ad, some of the questions can be answered by a simple phone call to the public relations or personnel department. Most will answer your questions honestly.

What assumptions can be made if you know the type of organization? Usually you can determine with considerable accuracy whether their recruiting policy is relatively flexible or very formalized, whether the personnel department handles the recruiting and hiring, whether you must follow a certain routine or if there is the opportunity to network, and how much time you probably have to submit your résumé.

The ads of each category of employer have certain distinct characteristics.

Private business   These ads are the most difficult to read because of the variety and the flexibility. You can assume that speed is important because there are no pressures, rules, or regulations requiring the employer to process your résumé in a specific manner or to even read it. It is not uncommon for companies to review résumés until they have an acceptable number of qualified candidates to interview and then disregard or discard the rest. You can also assume that your impression on the interviewer can carry more weight than your background because there usually are no formal procedures or formulas to assign numerical ratings to the amount of experience and education. You can also assume that the chances are greater that your résumé will be first screened by someone with little or no personnel experience. Clarity and simplicity are therefore of great importance.

Governmental entities   Although all organizations should operate under the general guidelines of equal employment opportunity guidelines, government entities are subject to a stricter set of rules. They design their hiring practices to achieve social goals as well as organizational goals. Consequently, such factors as veteran status, age, sex, and minority status can be given weight in the selection process. Your first step when applying for a government position is to contact the proper department and learn how that particular agency recruits, how the eligibility list is maintained, and if any factors are given preferential points or treatment. As a general rule, merely submitting a résumé is not sufficient to obtain an interview. You can assume, however, that time frames are not as critical as with private business. Most positions will have a closing date, and all applications or résumés received before that date will at least be read. We cannot overemphasize one point: learn how to conform to their procedures. The combination of regulations and political sensitivities usually results in a very rigidly enforced employment policy.

Public education   Public education is part of the governmental process and therefore subject to a very rigid employment procedure. However, there is usually less emphasis on the goals of society and more upon individual qualifications than in other governmental agencies, particularly at the college and university level. You will probably come into contact with that interesting phenomenon called the search committee, particularly for academic or professional staff positions. At the lower levels, department heads and section chiefs usually have more say over who is hired than other government agencies. Again, you can assume that you have more time because most positions have specific closing dates. You can also assume that the chance is great that your résumé will be read by someone in the department doing the hiring. It is also probable that your résumé will be processed according to strict equal opportunity guidelines, sometimes to the extent that any information concerning sex, age, marital status, religion, or ethnic origin will be blacked out or deleted. If you do not want your résumé to look like a patchwork quilt, do not provide any information concerning these issues.

Private business under contract to the government

A private business with many government contracts may have stipulations in those contracts that govern many of their recruiting and hiring practices. If you suspect that this may be the case, carefully check their recruiting and hiring system to be certain that you comply.

Applying to a large company

What assumptions can be made when considering the size? In a large company you can safely assume that you are dealing with large numbers of résumés for any advertised position. The larger corporations attract résumés like honey attracts bees. When they advertise, their ads run in several papers regionally or nationally. They often generate a response of five hundred to fifteen hundred résumés—occasionally as high as seven thousand. Aside from the fact that competition will be fierce, you can also deduce that the résumé-screening process will be accomplished in several stages. As far as you are concerned, the first screening is the most critical. It is usually done by a personnel check or a receptionist who compares the qualifications listed in the résumé with the advertised job description. Those who look like they meet the requirements go into one pile and those who don't go into another. The judgment is made according to information immediately available. The ads and the job descriptions are usually based on years of experience in certain jobs at certain levels; they require a stated minimum education or training level. If this information stands out in your résumé, you will survive the cut. If the clerk has to wade through four or five pages of material to determine your qualifications, your résumé will probably end up in the reject pile.

As a general rule, the larger the company, the less the knowledge about the position at the first screening level. The format and design of your résumé must take that fact into consideration. Remember also that, even in smaller companies, the first person to see your résumé will probably be a receptionist or a clerk. Either the résumé or the cover letter should clearly indicate the position that you are applying for so that the clerk can route the paper properly. Do not depend upon putting the name of the addressee on the envelope, because it is usually thrown away when opened.

Expect at least the possibility that, in a large company, the personnel or human resources department will be very turf conscious. The department will have specific procedures for receiving résumés under a variety of circumstances, such as mail, personal visits, and through other employees. Attempts to circumvent these procedures often result in the résumé's being discarded. So if you network, do it according to company rules.

Applying to a small company

In smaller companies, particularly those without an established personnel department, résumés are routed to the hiring department. Since the numbers are much fewer—sometimes as few as ten to twenty—there is a good chance that the hiring authority will review all résumés received. Although this fact does not eliminate the need for brevity and clarity, it does allow you more flexibility in the formulating of the résumé.

The initial evaluation

Who is responsible for the initial evaluation? The real question here is who further reduces the number of résumés after the initial screening? The hiring authority seldom sees more than twenty people. In some companies, the further reduction and evaluation is performed by the personnel department. In others, the hiring department may be responsible for both the initial and the final evaluation. If the personnel department performs the first evaluation, the actual person performing the function will be a skilled personnel specialist or assistant—skilled in personnel matters but not necessarily skilled in the requirements for the position in question. If your résumé is filled with technical terms and occupational buzzwords known only by those in your field, then you have a problem. Always write the basic portion of your résumé for a layperson. If technical information is necessary, submit it as an enclosure.

Affirmative action and equal opportunity

Is the organization subject to strict affirmative action and equal opportunity regulations? The question is, how strict is it? It is illegal for companies and organizations to ask questions about sensitive information. If you choose to provide it, most will accept it. Some organizations, however, will delete sensitive information before the résumé is sent to the hiring authority, while others will not even accept it. As a general rule, do not provide information concerning age, sex, marital status, race, or religion. Again, it is against the law for employers to ask for this information and unnecessary for you to provide it.

As a general rule, those with the strictest affirmative action and equal opportunity policies are government agencies, organizations under contract to government agencies, public educational institutions, and banks.

The recruiting and hiring function is an expensive process for any type or size of organization. This ever-increasing expense is responsible for a well-defined trend in employment practices that you should be aware of. More and more organizations are developing recruiting methods that avoid advertising job openings simply because of the time and expense involved in processing hundreds of résumés. As one director of human resources said:

> We will use every method possible to fill a position before we resort to advertising because of the extraordinary expense in both time and money. We will ask our employees to pass the word among their friends, we will give information about pending positions to professional associations, we are actively soliciting résumés on a continuing basis to provide a reservoir of potential employees when positions open, and we are structuring our labor force to be able to staff practically all of our middle- and upper-management and staff positions by promoting from within, thus limiting our recruiting efforts to entry-level positions—anything to avoid placing that ad.

There is little question about the fact that this trend will continue, and it certainly does not make your search any easier. The trend does, however, emphasize the importance of establishing contacts and networks.

Preparing Your Résumé

Before we begin the subject of preparing your résumé in detail, there are several comments that we should make about résumé writing in general.

General Tips on Résumé Writing

First impressions

Most people form first impressions of someone they have met very rapidly. These opinions or impressions may change later but only after considerable further contact. Résumés also create first impressions. In most cases your résumé has sold you or unsold you within the first fifteen seconds of reading, because the reader has created a first impression of you. The appearance, design, and construction of the résumé are very important. After all, it is the only thing that is marketing you, and the packaging is important. That is why manufacturers spend millions designing their soap packages.

Considering your reader

Most of the literature and lectures concentrate on preparing the résumé for the person who does the hiring. We can't argue with that logic, but it does not accommodate for the fact that getting a job by using a résumé is like playing professional sports—you can't play unless you survive the cuts. You can't get the job unless you survive the various stages of screening and evaluation. Usually fewer than ten people are actually interviewed for a position, regardless of how many résumés were received. The decision on whether you survive the cut is not made by the person doing the hiring. Therefore, you are also preparing that résumé for the clerk who opens the mail, the personnel clerk who compares your years of experience and education with the requirements outlined in the job description, the personnel assistant who evaluates the quality of your background, and possibly several other people.

Keeping it brief

Think of a person with a stack of résumés a foot high. He or she picks up yours—eight pages of closely typed narrative with information about your early childhood, your husband or wife and children, your hopes, your accomplishments and abilities, and on and on and on. Few people finish reading this type of résumé. The so-called résumé goes into the reject pile. Keep it brief and factual and don't lie. If you get the interview, you may not be able to remember what you lied about.

Designing for skimming

The term *skimming* refers to the fact that the person reviewing your résumé will not initially take the time to actually read it. He or she will glance over the first page and try to pick certain information and impressions: type of work, number of years, education, employment track (spotting dates to determine whether there are gaps in employment), and any other information that may be pertinent to the position. If the skimming produces a favorable first impression, the résumé will then be read or at least placed in the pile to be read.

The Three Types of Résumé Formats

Résumés differ from letters of application by virtue of the fact they are in an outline form rather than a narrative form. The outline form is designed to allow the reader to identify essential information without wading through the excess verbiage of the narrative style of writing.

The résumé outline itself can be arranged in three different formats: the chronological, the functional, or the combination. The primary difference among the three types is based on how the employment information is arranged and presented.

No style is best for all circumstances, although, for reasons outlined further on in this chapter, there is one style that is best suited for people changing careers or reentering the labor market. Your résumé has to do something for you that it does not have to do for people following a normal career progression. Your résumé has to show how your previous experience or educational background can be translated into your new career—how your background has prepared you, how your previous learning can be applied in your new direction. Your résumé has to convince the potential employer that your previous experience will be valuable in your new career. The better you can convince that employer, the better your chances of not only getting the job but also coming in higher than entry level.

The Outline Form of a Résumé

The outline form of a résumé aids the person screening for specific qualifications and experience. Within the top one-third of the page, this résumé establishes the objective, the number of years experience in the subject career field, essential skills, and the number of years of supervisory experience. By using various emphasizing techniques such as spacing, capitalization, underlining or, if you have the proper equipment, bold printing or variable type style, you highlight essential information so that it stands out and is easily read by someone skimming the text.

JANE E. JONES
4930 E. Lowell Road
Midtown, Ohio 12345
(111) 555-2233

Objective: A responsible position in the medical field involving administration and/or managerial functions.

Summary of Qualifications:
- Over ten years of accounting and office management experience in the medical and banking fields.
- Skills in typing (80 WPM), dictaphone transcription, computer operations, and independent correspondence. Also familiar with all types of insurance and collection procedures.
- Supervisory experience includes over eight years of training and employee evaluation.

Employment History:

1989 to present   Ear, Nose and Throat Center, Midtown, Ohio
Office Manager
Complete responsibility for all accounting with the exception of tax reporting. Duties include posting, billing, accounts payable and receivable utilizing a Digital VAX computer. Supervise eight employees and handle the medical transcription, correspondence, and accounting for the company and its pension plan.

1988 to 1989   Johnson Memorial Hospital, Midtown, Ohio
Office Coordinator
Provided administrative services to three ambulatory care centers. Performed general accounting including accounts receivable. Other duties included daily and monthly statistical reports and the periodic review and updating of policies and procedures. Conducted training classes for front office personnel.

(cont.)

1987 to 1988

General Medical Group Ltd., Midtown, Ohio
Office Manager
Responsible for accounts payable, accounts receivable, and data input for five physicians and a laboratory. Maintained six accounts from original posting through monthly and annual profit and loss statements. Initially hired as secretary to the business manager and subsequently promoted to office manager.

Concurrent w/above

United Way, Midtown, Ohio
Volunteer Bookkeeper
Designed, implemented, and maintained a bookkeeping system for a charitable foundation. System included a distribution tracking function for reporting purposes.

1985 to 1987

Midtown Health Foundation, Midtown, Ohio
Claims Manager
Responsible for claims approval, payment, member and provider relations, and the development of office systems and procedures. Originally hired as an office assistant making appointments and processing medical claims. Assumed position of claims manager in 1986.

Prior to 1985

Various duties involved in the classified advertising department of a local newspaper and as a teller, bookkeeper, and accounting clerk with the Midtown Bank and Trust Co.

Education: Mohawk County Community College, Midtown, Ohio.
Forty-one credit hours in accounting, bookkeeping, and business law (1980–1983)

References: Available upon request

The chronological résumé   Note that previously we stated that the styles differ in the manner of presenting the employment information. Such items as name, address, personal data, and educational data will usually be presented in the same way for all three styles, although the sequence can be arranged differently according to the relevancy or the type of industry.

The employment data is presented chronologically, beginning with the last or present employment and then working backward so that your first employment is listed last. Each employment period should be identified by the inclusive dates, the name of the organization, and a brief description of the duties and responsibilities. You may also include special projects, accomplishments such as sales volume statistics or start-up experience, or number of people supervised. Later on in this chapter we will comment on some alternative methods of presenting this type of information.

Sample Chronological Résumé

The following is an example of a chronological résumé. Note that the employment history is listed with the most current position placed first. It is perfectly acceptable in a chronological résumé to condense employment over ten or fifteen years old or employment that does not relate to your new career field. The placement of the education section depends upon its relevancy to your new field.

Jane E. Jones
2390 East Street
Midtown, Ohio 12345
(111) 555-2233

Objective: To obtain an administrative position offering challenge and the opportunity for advancement.

Employment History:

1989   First National Bank, Midtown, Ohio
               First and Second Mortgage Lender
               Part-time position with responsibilities in credit and collection, escrow, and secretarial duties.

1984 to 1988   Meridian Credit Corp., Midtown, Ohio
               Computer Terminal Operator
               Accounts receivable; assisted in collections; customer contact—personal and telephone; secretarial services.

               Credit Manager
               Supervised and implemented hands-on credit checking and verifications. Made credit decisions. Supervised and personally handled contract verification, discounting, purchase, and funding. Detailed month-end reports of credit decision ratios, purchase volume, etc. Personal and telephone contact with clients.

1979 to 1984   James Financial Services, Midtown, Ohio
               Personnel Benefits Administrator
               Created employee benefits orientation program complete with slides. Coordinated all miscellaneous benefits, e.g., carpool program, bus transit system, employee parking. Set up health and life insurance claims department. Received president's award for job performance.

(cont.)

Secretary to Director of Personnel
Operational Services Assistant
Airline travel coordinator for executives; policy and
procedures manual update and revisions; created
weekly company communications memo; editor of
company newsletter; interoffice mail program;
telephone communications assistant.

Word Processing Manager
Complete supervision of staff and equipment.
Responsible for study, recommendation, and proposal
for new systems. Prepared departmental budget
forecast every six months.

Education: Ames Community College, Midtown, Ohio
business administration, two years
Numerous seminars in personnel administration, business management, and word
processing.

References: Available upon request.

The functional résumé   In the functional résumé, your employment data is presented according to the type of experience, such as management, communications, sales, and marketing. The experience is not presented in relationship to any employer or date. If specific accomplishments are listed, these also are not necessarily attributed to a specific period. In the functional résumé, the employers and the dates of employment are sometimes listed, but they are not tied into the list of experience by function.

Sample Functional Résumé

The following is an example of a functional résumé. The person's employment history is categorized by function or job components. Note that you cannot relate the duties with the place of employment nor do you know how many years were spent at each position. As application for a position requiring a specific number of years experience, this résumé is useless. Note also that it is impossible to track the employment, thus preventing the reader from knowing whether or not the employment was continuous.

John T. Brown
1100 Eaton Street
Midtown, Ohio 12345
(111) 555-2233

Objective: A position involving managerial responsibilities in a heavy manufacturing industry.

Experience and Abilities:

Operations
Have been extensively involved in production operations including scheduling, expediting, and quality control. Through effective planning and scheduling, I increased productivity in the manufacture of truck transmissions by 28 percent.

Purchasing
Supervised the purchasing function of raw materials and parts in a heavy equipment repair facility. Improved receiving procedures and computerized the purchase order and specifications system.

Inventory Control
Developed an inventory control system classified by manufacturer (parts). Coordinated parts requirements with both long-term and short-term planning. Installed a computerized perpetual inventory system.

Managerial
Have supervised six to twenty-one employees in a manufacturing environment. Extensive experience in labor relations involving the machinists union. Responsible for short-term planning, scheduling, staffing, and quality control.

Problem Solving
Have served on production planning committees for over three years. Although most of the planning involved new production lines, often we were assigned to solve problems in existing manufacturing procedure that decreased product rejects by 80 percent.

Employment History: Olson Truck Manufacturing Inc., Midtown, Ohio
International Heavy Equipment, Midtown, Ohio
Paramount Manufacturing, Midtown, Ohio

Education: Ohio University, B.S. in Production Engineering

References: Available upon request.

The combination résumé   As the name implies, this style is a combination of the functional and chronological. Usually, the résumé features a functional section first, in which the experience is summarized by function. Education can also be summarized in this section if it is relevant. The employment is then listed in reverse chronological order with the most recent listed first.

Sample Combination Résumé

The following is an example of a combination résumé. It combines the functional experience and skills in the summary and then goes on to the chronological listing of work experience and education. The summary usually lists the experience and the skills in the same type of language as most ads describe the position requirements. The combination style is most adapted to use in career change situations because the summary section can be used to highlight those skills and experiences that are most translatable to the new career direction.

Jane E. Jones
2300 East Street
Midtown, Ohio 12345
(111) 555-2233

Objective: To obtain a position involving considerable public service contact or sales with the potential for management-level responsibilities.

Summary of Qualifications:

Over eight years of successful and progressive experience in positions of responsibility involving sales, customer service, and customer relations.

An effective supervisor with excellent skills in verbal and written communication, organization, and motivation. Adept at statistics and analysis.

Versatile, flexible, and career oriented. Proven ability to function well independently and deal with the public in a positive and professional manner.

Employment History:
June 1984–December 1989

Holiday Resort Systems, Midtown, Ohio
Reservations Supervisor
Responsible for the supervision of ten to sixteen reservation agents at the national telephone center of an organization of international resorts. Provide information as to new procedure formats, new facilities, and new computer formats. Compile productivity statistics for submission to the reservation manager and implement employee evaluations. Troubleshoot all problems. Extensive international travel, frequently acting as tour guide for travel agents to acquaint them with the facilities. Initially hired as a reservations agent, promoted to reservations coordinator and subsequently to supervisor.

(cont.)

1982–1984	Harrigan's Department Store, Midtown, Ohio **Sales** Assisted in design and sales of fine and unique jewelry. Responsible for displays, floor merchandising, and small repairs. Assisted in buying.
Previous Experience:	Numerous positions in sales and customer service including assistant manager of the Spaghetti Company.

Education: University of Toledo, Toledo, Ohio
liberal arts, two years
Seminars
Xerox—professional sales skills
Max Sacks International—professional sales skills
American Management Association—professional management skills

Analyzing the Three Styles

Both the chronological and the functional formats have advantages and disadvantages from the viewpoints of both the potential employer and employee.

The chronological résumé is most commonly used probably because it is the easiest and most logical to assemble. It is a historical presentation and requires little creativity to write the statements of experience. Although it may be the easiest to read, it is the most difficult to screen and evaluate. For example, if the résumé is used as an application for a position requiring a minimum number of years in several different functions, the person doing the screening must do the arithmetic necessary to determine whether or not you are qualified. If your work background is varied and the new job's requirements are complex and detailed, the personnel assistant doing the screening may not take the time and trouble. The chronological résumé can also present the job hopper in an unfavorable light as well as the person who has unexplained or illogical gaps in employment. Obviously this type of employment history will be much more of a problem for a man than for a woman. In the case of a married or divorced woman reentering or changing careers, these gaps are expected and are not viewed in an unfavorable light.

The functional résumé gained popularity in the sixties and seventies as the professional employment agencies and counselors gained in numbers and influence. They found that the functional approach was the most flexible style and could adapt to many different situations, including those clients with problem employment histories. Some agencies found that the functional format was also the easiest to sell to the client.

The functional is the easiest to screen, but only if the number of years of experience are included in the function statements. If the number of years is not included, then the functional résumé is almost impossible to interpret. For example, it is hard to evaluate a résumé if the position description requires "Ten years in sales management at the regional level," and the résumé merely states, "highly skilled as a regional sales manager." Obviously, under these circumstances, the résumé will be tossed into the reject pile.

It would appear on the surface that the functional résumé would be most appropriate for those of you seeking to reenter or change careers. You have greater flexibility to pick out those areas of your previous work history that are relevant to your new career direction and highlight them in the appropriate functional breakdowns. We would agree and perhaps recommend the functional in many cases except for one very important fact. Forty-eight personnel and human resource professionals of diverse backgrounds and industries were asked about their preferences as to résumé style. All but one indicated that they did not like the functional style. Some of the reasons given were, "very difficult to evaluate experience," "almost impossible to verify," "the format is used to hide too many problems," and "difficult to determine employment continuity." Based on these responses, we recommend that the functional style should not be used under any circumstances.

The combination résumé has the advantages of both and the disadvantages of neither; consequently, we recommend this style in practically every instance involving career change and reentry. One might argue that the combination résumé should not be used in a situation involving a thirty-five-year-old woman entering the labor market with no previous employment. Under these and similar situations, any type of résumé is not appropriate. A simple letter of application with relevant personal data and educational background is far more effective.

The combination résumé still has the flexibility to be adapted to new career direction. It still provides the necessary employment track and allows the reader to relate duties with dates and companies. Some of you may be concerned that you cannot hide the fact that you are changing careers or that you are reentering the work force if you use a combination-type résumé. You will have to face the fact that you cannot hide your situation under any circumstances. If it is not obvious in the résumé, the information will come out in the interview. Most potential employers will resent the fact that there are big surprises developing as you are questioned about your background. As we mentioned in the very beginning of this book, your situation is very commonplace. Most employers are very sophisticated in accepting applications from people reentering or changing careers. You should be entirely upfront about your situation to avoid any misconceptions or surprises. We will make some other suggestions about how to accomplish this in the section about cover letters.

Sample Résumé for Changing Careers or Reentry

This résumé states as an objective the intention to change careers or reenter the job market. It is designed to form a more positive and receptive attitude on the part of the reader by channeling attention to the translatable skills.

Jane E. Jones
2300 East Street
Midtown, Ohio 12345
(111) 555-2233

Objective:	To effect a change in career direction by obtaining a position in the travel industry.
Summary of Qualifications:	• Over ten years experience in customer service and sales. • Excellent skills in verbal and written communications. • Travel school graduate.

Employment History:

1986 to 1989	Mack Distributors, Midtown, Ohio **Sales and Distribution Representative** Represented a line of products designed for children and manufactured in California. Responsible for sales, warehousing, and distribution. Maintained excellent customer relations by providing fast and efficient service resulting in a 94 percent repeat order ratio. Handled as many as 150 accounts.
1978 to 1985	Everett Title Company, Midtown, Ohio **Assistant Escrow Officer** Heavy phone and personal contact with customers, appraisers, and lending institutions. Prepared legal documents for brokers and developers and coordinated closings.
Education:	Wheaton College, Norton, Massachusetts liberal arts–2 years University of California at Los Angeles business, merchandising, and marketing–1½ years International Institute of Travel, Phoenix, Arizona.

Personal:
Current address: 999 Eve Avenue, Midtown, Ohio, 12345
Telephone: (111) 555-2233
References: Available upon request

Constructing Your Personal History

The assumption is being made that, at this point, you have read and followed the instructions and suggestions in the preceding chapters. Having chosen your goals and having prepared yourself emotionally and mentally to begin this new direction are absolutely essential if you are to be successful in obtaining the type of employment you desire. The majority of people are not mentally, emotionally, or intellectually prepared either to reenter the workforce or to change careers. You are about to make a significant change. It will require a high degree of objectivity and an understanding of who you are and what your strengths and weaknesses are.

At this stage you will need to return to the lists that you prepared previously. You will now use these lists in conjunction with other information to compile a résumé worksheet. This résumé worksheet is designed to contain the following information even though much of this information will not be used in the résumé.

Education and training

Enter the school names, dates, major and minor fields of emphasis, and other subject areas involving fifteen credit hours or more. Include high schools, two- and four-year colleges and universities, graduate schools, technical and vocational schools, military schools, and correspondence schools.

Enter seminars, in-house training programs, specialized courses, certification programs or courses, or specialized equipment training.

Employment

Unlike the résumé, begin with your first part-time employment regardless of the duration. Enter the name of the employing organization or person, your duties and responsibilities, your contact with others outside, and your supervisors. Enter the inclusive dates of your employment.

As a separate category, enter special accomplishments, projects, temporary assignments, your likes and dislikes about the job, and why you left.

Continue to list every period of employment using the same format and providing the same information until you reach the present.

Volunteer or nonpaid activities

Enter the names, dates, and activities performed and include the names of people with whom you came in contact, both volunteers and those employed by the volunteer organization. Itemize your accomplishments and particularly note those functions that you were good at and enjoyed.

Nonoccupational activities

List hobbies and other interests. Many nonoccupational activities require the development of skills that have a definite application to certain types of occupations. For example, skills are gained from belonging to Toastmasters International (public speaking), building and racing cars, writing, or developing different programs and functions on your personal computer.

Although most counselors and authors recommend some type of a résumé worksheet in a format similar to the one described above, you will be using the worksheet in a slightly different manner.

Also, list the functions involved in each period of employment, volunteer, and nonoccupational activity; however, you will have to take a further step because of your status as one who is changing your career or reentering or both.

Usually your worksheet will contain such functions as management or supervisory experience, retail sales, recordkeeping, typing, computer operations, engineering, and machine operation. If you have had several jobs spanning a period of fifteen years or more, it would not be unusual for you to have been involved in twenty or thirty different job functions. Your next move is to identify those job functions that will translate or are transferable to your new career goals. As you review the functions, either mark the appropriate functions in red or make a separate list. Give considerable thought to your choices because you will be using this information in three ways: first, you may use some items in your cover letter; second, you will be listing some items in the functional section of your résumé; and third, you will be emphasizing these functions in the chronological section of your employment history.

The Résumé Worksheet

Although you will be using this worksheet extensively during the preparation of your résumé, the organization of this work will differ markedly from your résumé format. The goal in the design of this worksheet is to reconstruct your occupational life as it actually developed, starting with your first job, no matter how seemingly insignificant, and progressing through to your most recent. Detail and completeness is important now. Save your brevity and condensing for the actual résumé preparation.

You will note that you are asked to evaluate how your attitudes and psychological profile met the demands of each job—what type of person did each job require in terms of personality and character? For example, did the job require creativity, stress tolerance, perseverance, detail, tolerance about repetitive activities, people skills, extroversion? How well did you meet those requirements? There is a specific reason for asking you to perform this evaluation. There is, in many industries today, a tendency to rely heavily on psychological testing when matching people to positions. Increasingly, job specifications, a description of the type of person needed, are being used in conjunction with job descriptions that tend to emphasize required skills, experience, and education for the position.

Your time and effort spent in preparing these worksheets will pay off not only in the preparation of your résumé but also as you prepare for an interview.

Work Experience

Job title _____

Organization _____ Supervisor _____

From _____ to _____

Chronology of duties from beginning the job until leaving:

_____

_____

_____

_____

_____

_____

_____

_____

_____

_____

What skills did you learn?

_____

_____

_____

_____

_____

What did you like most about the job? _____

_____

_____

What did you dislike about the job? _____

_____

_____

What type of person would be best to do this job? _____

_____

_____

What personality requirements did you meet or not meet? _____

_____

_____

Work Experience

Job title _____

Organization _____ Supervisor _____

From _____ to _____

Chronology of duties from beginning the job until leaving:

_____

_____

_____

_____

_____

_____

_____

_____

_____

_____

What skills did you learn?

_____

_____

_____

_____

_____

What did you like most about the job? _____

_____

_____

What did you dislike about the job? _____

_____

_____

What type of person would be best to do this job? _____

_____

_____

What personality requirements did you meet or not meet? _____

_____

_____

Work Experience

Job title _____

Organization _____ Supervisor _____

From _____ to _____

Chronology of duties from beginning the job until leaving:

_____

_____

_____

_____

_____

_____

_____

_____

_____

What skills did you learn?

_____

_____

_____

_____

What did you like most about the job? _____

_____

_____

What did you dislike about the job? _____

_____

_____

What type of person would be best to do this job? _____

_____

_____

What personality requirements did you meet or not meet? _____

_____

_____

Work Experience

Job title _____

Organization _____ Supervisor _____

From _____ to _____

Chronology of duties from beginning the job until leaving:

_____

_____

_____

_____

_____

_____

_____

_____

_____

_____

_____

What skills did you learn?

_____

_____

_____

_____

_____

What did you like most about the job? _____

_____

_____

What did you dislike about the job? _____

_____

_____

What type of person would be best to do this job? _____

_____

_____

What personality requirements did you meet or not meet? _____

_____

_____

Work Experience

Job title _____

Organization _____ Supervisor _____

From _____ to _____

Chronology of duties from beginning the job until leaving:

_____

_____

_____

_____

_____

_____

_____

_____

_____

_____

What skills did you learn?

_____

_____

_____

_____

_____

What did you like most about the job? _____

_____

_____

What did you dislike about the job? _____

_____

_____

What type of person would be best to do this job? _____

_____

_____

What personality requirements did you meet or not meet? _____

_____

_____

EDUCATION

High school   Name _____ Dates _____

Address _____

_____

Major _____

Best classes _____

Extracurricular activities _____

College or   1. _____ Dates _____
tech school
2. _____ Dates _____

3. _____ Dates _____

Majors _____

_____

Best subjects _____

Extracurricular activities _____

Graduate   1. _____ Dates _____
schools
2. _____ Dates _____

Seminars and   _____
courses
_____

_____

_____

_____

_____

_____

_____

_____

_____

VOLUNTEER ACTIVITIES AND ORGANIZATION MEMBERSHIP

Organization _____ Dates _____

Activities _____

_____

Skills learned _____

_____

Possible contacts _____

_____

Organization _____ Dates _____

Activities _____

_____

Skills learned _____

_____

Possible contacts _____

_____

Organization _____ Dates _____

Activities _____

_____

Skills learned _____

_____

Possible contacts _____

_____

Organization _____ Dates _____

Activities _____

_____

Skills learned _____

_____

Possible contacts _____

_____

Equipment and Special Projects

Equipment skills. List the types of equipment skills you have mastered—computers, machines, vehicles.

_____

_____

_____

_____

_____

_____

_____

_____

_____

Special Projects. List the projects that you have completed as part of your past jobs or volunteer/political/organizational activities.

_____

_____

_____

_____

_____

_____

_____

_____

_____

Note: These items are probably most appropriately listed as résumé addendums or inserts.

OBJECTIVES

After reviewing your occupational, educational, and activity history, list below all the job objectives that you would qualify for. Then eliminate those positions that do not interest you. Next eliminate those that you feel do not meet your personality and psychological profile.

_____

_____

_____

_____

_____

_____

_____

_____

_____

_____

_____

_____

_____

_____

_____

_____

_____

_____

_____

_____

_____

SUMMARY OF QUALIFICATIONS

Review your past work experience, your education, and experience gained in other activities. Separate these experiences into functions or categories. Now list those separate functions in terms of type of experience, level of experience, and length of time whenever possible. For example, "Over nine years experience as a production control supervisor"; "ten years experience in the marketing and sales of plastic consumer goods."

_____

_____

_____

_____

_____

_____

_____

_____

_____

_____

_____

_____

_____

_____

_____

_____

_____

_____

_____

Constructing the Résumé

There is, at this point, considerable discussion of whether this type of personal document should be titled *Résumé* or some other title such as *Brief of Qualifications*. Since the word *Résumé* is now commonly understood to refer to a personal employment and personal history including qualitative statements about your abilities and strengths, either title is acceptable. However, note that the majority of ads still ask for a résumé. For purposes of convenience, we will continue to call the document a *Résumé*.

Type of paper and type style

Always use a high quality twenty-pound or twenty-four pound bond paper. The color should be white or a very light shade of beige, blue, or green. Darker shades, textured paper, or other decorative gimmicks are not advisable unless such design features are part of the presentation, as in the case of a graphic artist. The size of the paper is always 8½ by 11 inches or 11 by 17 inches folded in half. Résumés involving more than one page can be assembled in loose-leaf form, brochure form (11 by 17 inches folded to make an 8½ by 11-inch folder), or bound with spirals. The brochure form is handy if you have information on additional inserts such as salary history, references, special projects, or publications that you may not want to send to every prospective employer. The spiral form is most appropriate for those in the academic or scientific-technical community, whose résumés usually include lists of published works, papers, presentations, and research projects.

How many pages?

Over and over again we hear that a résumé should never be more than one page. Seldom, however, do we hear this from the employers. The résumé should be long enough to provide the essential data about you—keeping in mind the rule of brevity and clarity. As a general rule, however, the basic résumé should be no longer than two pages; any further detail should be included as inserts and addendums. The summary of your qualifications, your work history, and your education should be limited to the basic two pages. If additional information is needed—such as your sales accomplishments, special projects that you have been involved in, or the types of specialized equipment you have used—then provide that information on separate addendums or inserts. Why? Keep in mind the screening process: convince the reader that you are qualified on the first two pages and then furnish the information that is meaningful only to the hiring authority on the additional pages.

Type style   Do not get too "cute" with the type style. There are several standard styles that are easily read, but there are many others that are very difficult to scan. Certainly some characteristics that highlight are acceptable, even desirable, if they aid in scanning or skimming to pick out the essential information. Such characteristics include blocking, overstriking, capitalizing, and underlining. Having your résumé typeset is not absolutely necessary, particularly since the new electronic typewriters and word processors have the flexibility to highlight by varying the type size and style. Copier technology is such that high-quality copies can be produced that are almost indistinguishable from typeset printed copies.

Should your résumé be professionally prepared?   Certainly it is advisable to have a résumé professionally typed. But before you go to a résumé counseling service, there are a few things about these operations that you should know. First check the credentials of the person who will be actually preparing your résumé. Has the preparer had experience both in writing and in general personnel work? Is he or she familiar with hiring practices and processes? Résumé services range from very bad to very good. Some are part of national or regional chains, and others are one-person local operations. Many services advertise that they are trained in counseling and preparation when, in many cases, the only training they received is how to sell résumés. Finding a competent person or service is usually a matter of shopping the field and having good luck.

Should you enclose a picture of yourself?   As a general rule, you should absolutely not enclose your picture. Some potential employers would construe the picture as an effort to circumvent equal opportunity regulations. What is the exception to the rule? You should enclose a picture if you are applying for a job in modeling, acting, or entertainment.

Sample Loose-Leaf Two-Page Résumé

The following is an example of a loose-leaf two-page résumé for someone who has had three or four significant positions.

James E. Jones
1234 Brown Street
Midtown, Ohio 12345
(111) 555-2233

Career Goal:	Responsible general management position utilizing experience in contracts, marketing, and customer support.
Summary of Qualifications:	• Nineteen years of progressive experience in contract negotiation, marketing, and customer support primarily in management-level positions. • Considerable marketing experience involving both public and private sectors. • Demonstrated effectiveness in total program development.
Experience: April 1989 to present	Paramont Aviation, Midtown, Ohio **TFE731 Turbofan Jet Engine International Customer Support Program Manager** Account Responsibilities: 　Gates Learjet Model 35/55 Program 　Cessna Citation III Program 　Casa C101 Program (Spain) 　Chinese Air Force AT3 Program (Taiwan) 　U.S. Air Force C21A and U.S. Navy 　　CT39/Proposal Manager Management responsibility for total logistics program consisting of support contract negotiation; initial spares procurement; tooling and test equipment; product training; service personnel; customer symposium presentations; single point customer contact.

April 1986 to April 1989	Johnson Manufacturing, Midtown, Ohio **Warranty Manager, Customer Support** Product: high technology jet/prop gas turbine engines, airline auxiliary power units and pneumatic control and start systems for domestic and international markets. Supervised four administrators, including one staff member in Europe, working within a $35 million annual budget and reporting directly to the office president in charge of customer support. Achievements include creation of winning contract guarantee program for Boeing 757/767 Program and the implementation of computerized incident value warranty forecasting technique.

November 1984 to April 1986	Gorman Industries, Midtown, Ohio
	Contract Manager, International Programs
	Responsibility: $25 million annually.
	Product: gas turbine auxiliary power units.
	Complete contract management for major product sales consisting of the following:
	    product pricing
	    terms and conditions
	    negotiations
	    contract performance

August 1974 to November 1984	Acme Environmental Systems Division Torrance, California **Contract Administrator, International and Domestic Programs** Responsibility: $25 million multidivisional programs for commercial, international, and government markets. Product: environmental control and air-conditioning systems.
Education:	University of California at Los Angeles International business course work–1983 Government contract management–degree, 1981 University of Southern California MBA courses in marketing, 1973–1976 University of San Diego Bachelor of science degree in marketing, 1973 double minor—economics/philosophy
Affiliations:	National Contract Management Association—1980 International Customer Service Association—1984

Sample Two-Page Brochure

The following is an example of a two-page brochure format. This type of presentation is most often used when there may be a variety of inserts—salary history, references, projects, equipment—or any other information that you may not want to send to every job prospect.

John Prescott
1234 East Road
Midtown, Ohio 12345
(111) 555-2233

Objective:

To obtain a position as chief engineer, general manager, or in technical sales, preferably in aviation or a related industry.

Summary of Qualifications:

Thirty years experience in management, engineering, and project engineering.

Considerable experience in estimating, preparation of bid proposals, and negotiations through prebid to final award.

Extensive design experience in mechanicals, hydraulics, power wiring, and control circuits.

Strong background as project manager in various testing functions relating to military and commercial aviation.

Employment History:
June 1987 to present

Consultant
Provide design and consulting service relating to Energy Management Systems and Hydraulic Test Equipment to commercial and industrial clients.

January 1984 to June 1987

Mayfield Engineering, Midtown, Ohio
Chief Engineer
Coordinated efforts for formal identification system for computerized inventory. Initiated work order program for machine shop and assembly department to assist in production scheduling. Supervised the design and evaluation of products relating to the construction industry.

September 1982 to November 1983	Jones Technical Services, Midtown, Ohio **Designer** Designed stationary and portable (mobile) hydraulic test stands and automotive maintenance benches. Developed operational, maintenance, and servicing manuals. Supervised draftspeople on specific design projects. Conducted three-day training seminar at U.S. Coast Guard ATC, Mobile, Alabama. Designed and tested hydraulic servicing unit for *Air Force One*. Projects involved both military and commercial applications.
October 1980 to September 1982	Press Aviation, Midtown, Ohio **Test Engineer** Set up facility to test overhauled jet engine fuel controls, designed test fixtures to accommodate new components, modified existing test benches for additional units, and demonstrated test procedures on test rigs to bench aircraft mechanics.
Prior to 1980	Various positions in engineering and management including: Twelve years as **chief engineer** supervising engineers and draftspeople in the design of stationary, portable, and mobile equipment used by various branches of the military. Processed all bids (IFBs) and contract production orders and coordinated with quality control on all prototype and production testing. Five years as **senior project engineer** in the development of hydraulic and pneumatic test stands. Five years as **project engineer** designing hydraulic test stands.
Related Duties:	Most of the above-listed positions involved considerable on-site engineering and design work modifying existing equipment to accommodate new components and performing field installations.
Education:	Michigan Technological University B.S. degree in Mechanical Engineering
Personal:	Security Clearance: Top Secret Military: U.S. Navy References: Available upon request

Composing the Résumé   The information contained in a résumé should be grouped by topic or classification and presented in an outline form. For example, most résumés will contain some or all of the following classifications of information:

- Personal information
- Job or career objective
- General statement of qualifications
- Employment history
- Education
- Salary history
- References
- Professional organizations, committees, associations
- Publications, presentations, lectures, or seminars (as a speaker)
- Special projects: research, technical, job related
- Specialized equipment—computers, vehicles, and machinery
- Certifications, honors, and awards
- Nonoccupational activities—hobbies, community service, volunteer work
- Job-related training programs, seminars, and courses attended

You have considerable flexibility as to how and in what sequence you present the information in your résumé. Common sense should dictate that the information be arranged logically. That is, the general job description should come before any details referring to the job, the general statement of qualifications can be tracked in the employment history section. However, keep in mind that you are arranging this information for several people—the initial screener, the evaluator, and the final hiring authority.

Title   Enter the title at the top of the first page or, when preparing a brochure or bound résumé, on the cover page—résumé, brief of qualifications, qualifications brief, personal and employment history—whatever you think is the most appropriate title.

Name   Enter your current name as it appears on payroll or personnel records and bank accounts. Do not use nicknames, such as Charles "Chuck" Jones or Elizabeth "Betsy"

Brown. Most women, because of marriage and sometimes divorce, will have had two or more legal names during their adult life. If your name was different at the time you were employed than it is now, then enter the information just after your job title in the employment history section. If your degree is important to the job and would probably be verified, then enter your legal name at the time of your degree in the education section.

Address and telephone number
This is usually the next item of information furnished unless you are in a transient situation. If you are in transit, it is appropriate to furnish this information in the cover letter or as an insert or addendum.

Personal data
You should not furnish your sex, age, marital status, height, weight, health, and date and place of birth. By law, employers are not allowed to ask for this information but will accept it if furnished. However, some will either delete this information or refuse to accept the résumé. Remember, employers are becoming increasingly sensitive to their exposure to discrimination claims—if the information is not furnished, they cannot be accused of being biased in their screening procedures. Under certain circumstances, employers can ask for some personal data if it can be proven that knowledge of the data is essential to the selection process. In those cases, the nature of the job might demand certain physical, sex, or age characteristics.

Objective
In most instances, particularly in a career change or reentry situation, the job or career objective should be stated. The objective may be stated in either specific or general terms. It is usually also advisable to be direct about the fact that your objective is the result of a desire to reenter the job market or change your career direction. You may state your situation in the objective section or in the cover letter or both. You should be very direct about your intentions in order to create an open mind on the part of the reader and to eliminate any questions or surprises that may result in a negative impression. You should understand that without prior knowledge of your purpose for applying, a potential employer will naturally wonder why you are applying for the position with your background. If

the reader is forewarned, he or she will interpret your background in a more positive light and consciously look for translatable skills. Again, it is a matter of creating the proper first impression.

The question as to how specific you should be in your objective statement can be answered by identifying how the résumé is to be used. If it is to be used an an application for only one position or a limited number of positions, then you can be very specific about your direction. If you plan to use the résumé in a variety of situations, then your objective should be general, and you should use the cover letter to direct the résumé to specific positions.

The use of superlatives in the objective should be avoided. For example, avoid saying "a position utilizing my superb organizational skills." As one human resource director said, "It is difficult enough to get an accurate picture of the applicant, but it is virtually impossible if I have to wade through a bunch of self-glorifying garbage."

You can also use a multiple objective if your goals are naturally related in the industry. "A position as an electronics technician or a materials expediter" may not be appropriate, but "A position as an operations supervisor or project manager" might be acceptable.

Sample Résumé with Specific Objective

The following is an example of a résumé with a specific objective and an outline that emphasizes the maintenance function in a specific industry—plastics and molding. The language is designed to reinforce the objective by using action verbs and nouns that relate.

John H. Jones
2130 Center Street
Midtown, Ohio 12345
(111) 555-2233

Objective:	To obtain a position as a maintenance supervisor in an industry involved in plastics and molding.
Summary of Qualifications:	• Twelve years of experience in plastics including injection molding, blow molding, vacuum forming, compression molding, and transfer molding. • Over nine years managerial experience with a proven ability to relate well to all levels of personnel. • A successful inventor, having one final patent and four pending.

Employment History:

1986–1988 1989–present	Morton Plastics, Midtown, Ohio **Assistant Manager (Maintenance)** Responsible for machine maintenance and product quality control. Scheduled production and assisted in tool design. Currently supervise six machine operators. Initially hired as maintenance supervisor and subsequently promoted to assistant manager. I left the company temporarily in 1988 when it was sold and, by request, returned in 1989.
1988 to 1989	Brown Manufacturing, Midtown, Ohio **Assistant Supervisor** Maintained, rebuilt, and improved machinery used in vacuum forming. Acted as shift supervisor and was responsible for supervising machine set-ups.
1984 to 1986	Jackson Manufacturing, Midtown, Ohio **Assistant Manager** (Injection and Blow Molding) Originally hired in machine maintenance and promoted to assistant manager two months later. Supervised a production staff of six.
Prior to 1984	Held several positions in maintenance and maintenance supervision involving injection, transfer, and compression molding.
Education:	Midtown Technical Institute, Midtown, Ohio. Plastics engineering—1½ years.
References:	Available upon request

The summary or statement of qualifications

We can describe the relationship among the objective, the summary of qualifications, and the employment history as follows: "The objective tells where you want to go, the summary tells that you are qualified to go there, and the employment history proves it."

When developing your summary of qualifications, return to the part of your résumé worksheet where you identified the functions in each position and selected those that related to your current career direction. If you performed similar functions in several jobs, then add up the total amount of time in each function. Compose two to six brief statements summarizing your experience by function or position. Whenever possible, state the number of years in that function or position. Also indicate any facts that demonstrate success. If a certain level or type of education is normally required for the desired position, then state your level and the major or emphasis if appropriate. Identify any areas of specialty, for example, "Four years specializing in labor relations and contract negotiations." Use position titles if appropriate, for example, "Eight years experience as a property manager supervising apartment complexes, office facilities, and shopping malls."

Remember also that one of the principal functions of the summary of qualifications is to make the task of screening the résumé easier for the person who must use a list of minimum qualifications to determine whether you are qualified to stay in the running. If the summary is constructed properly, you will have established your qualifications within the first half or third of the first page.

Education

This section can follow either the summary of qualifications or the employment history. The decision as to where to place it is based on the importance of your education to your career objective. If your education is a significant requirement for the job, then place it after the summary. If your job experience is more significant, then place the education section after your employment history.

If you attended more than one college or university before graduating, then listing the degree-granting institution is usually sufficient since that institution has usually accepted your previous course work as transfer credits. The exception to this rule would be attendance at a school in which you majored in subjects other than your final field of concentration, particularly if these courses are important to your career objective.

You should list the name of the institution, the location,

and your field of concentration or your major and minor. The date of graduation is not necessary. If your name was different when you graduated, give your name as listed on the transcripts to facilitate verification of your credentials. Extracurricular activities are not usually listed unless they have a significant bearing on your career direction.

Important seminars, training programs, certifications, and licenses can also be listed in this section as well as any postgraduate, nondegree courses.

Employment history   Your employment history should be listed beginning with your current or most recent employment and then working backward to your first. List the inclusive dates for each period of employment, the name of the company or organization, the city and state, the title of your position, and, if different now, your legal name while employed. If you had several positions with the same company, list the last position held in the heading and then identify the other positions in the body of the job description. Describe your functions using action verbs as much as possible: supervised, developed, maintained. Use numbers: number of people supervised, beginning and ending sales volume, number of clients. Again, using your résumé worksheet, emphasize those functions relating to your new career direction. Double-check to ensure that you have listed those functions used in your summary of qualifications. Be certain to list those accomplishments showing initiative and imagination such as start-ups and special projects. Remember again—brevity and clarity—you are writing a résumé, not an autobiography.

In many cases you can list your last ten to fifteen years of employment in the format outlined here. Then under the heading Prior to 19XX, write a summation of your work experience prior to that date.

Gaps in employment pose a problem in some cases. Women whose work history shows gaps during the years they brought up a family usually have no problem because these gaps are expected. Men and women having periods of being involuntarily unemployed may have a problem in employment continuity. This problem is best handled in the employment interview, if possible. It is best to be truthful because it is better to have not obtained the position in the first place than to be released or fired after having been caught in a lie.

People with problem work histories have a better chance of obtaining employment through networking and contacts than through classified ads or shotgunning.

Nonoccupational interests and hobbies, community and volunteer services

Although in the past it has been customary to include such information as hobbies and other interests, it is now generally accepted that this information is only included if it has some relevancy to the position sought. For example, you would want to state that your hobbies were fishing, baseball, and football if you were applying for a position as a sales representative for a sporting goods company. Often people changing careers or reentering the work force will choose occupational areas that are closely allied to a former hobby or interest. A case in point involved a former business executive who built and raced cars for a hobby for over twenty years. He applied for and was accepted as a regional manager for a chain of custom auto parts stores.

Community and volunteer services are often very important to those of you reentering or seeking employment after a long-term involvement with social service groups working with other volunteers. In fact, if your involvement was on a regular basis, part-time or full-time, then it is perfectly acceptable to include this experience under the employment history section. For example, one woman who had been on the board of directors of a charitable foundation had been responsible for organizing fund drives to support a museum, establishing and operating a crisis center for abused children, and maintaining a hot line for drug counseling. Often she would be organizing and supervising as many as eighty volunteers. The fact that she was not paid for these activities was immaterial. Using these activities as part of a summary of qualifications and a work history, she soon found a position as a director of a nonprofit community service group that paid her a substantial salary.

Organizing and supervising volunteers has become a very marketable skill as the number of privately and publicly funded social service organizations has increased considerably during the past two decades. In fact, several people who started as volunteers eventually obtained paid positions with such organizations as the Girl Scouts, the senior citizens center, and even a trade association.

Salary history

It is strongly suggested that your previous history never be included in your basic résumé. Review the classified section of your newspaper and you will notice that a salary history is only requested in about 30 to 50 percent of the ads. Why furnish information that may affect your chances for an interview if it is not requested? Type up your salary history on a separate sheet of paper. Include it in your résumé packet as an insert or enclosure only if it is requested. Obviously the subject of salary has to be approached at some point, but the most opportune time is during or after the preliminary interview. Remember also that, as a career changer or someone involved in reentry, your salary history is not as relevant as it is in a situation involving someone applying for a position in their normal job progression. If a salary history is requested, then you should acknowledge the fact that it is relatively unimportant in your cover letter and that you would wish to negotiate salary based on your present circumstances. By using this approach, you can eliminate any preconceived salary expectations based on your previous positions, a perception that could eliminate you from the preliminary interview.

Inserts and enclosures   It has been recommended previously that the basic résumé be no longer than two pages. However, many of you have special experiences or skills that must be itemized or described for evaluation by the hiring authority. This information should be included as a separate category because of its complexity. This information will mean very little to the people initially screening the résumé and, in fact, would tend only to obscure the details of your basic experience. Examples of the types of specialized information to be included as inserts are as follows:

- Professional organizations, committees, associations, and societies: Include the name of the organization, your position or positions, special committees, and length of service.
- Publications, presentations, lectures, and seminars (as speaker): List the title of the article or presentation, for whom it was presented, the title of the publication, and the dates.
- Special projects: research, technical, job related: This is perhaps one of the most important categories, because in this section you can highlight any special jobs or projects in which you excelled. Projects in a résumé context refer to assignments ranging from one-time duties performed as part of your normal job to responsibilities involving a well-defined task, such as

the construction of a particular building or a specific market study. The project approach is particularly appropriate for those in the engineering field or research and development.

- Specialized equipment: Many of you in computers, construction, transportation, manufacturing, and accounting have had the opportunity to become skilled in the use of various types of equipment. In some instances, a list of these equipment items should be provided to the prospective employer. Bear in mind, however, that this list may work against you if it does not include equipment currently used by the prospect.
- Certifications, awards and honors: Although, in most cases, certifications, awards, and honors are listed under the education section if they are academic in nature, many are also occupation related and can be listed separately, especially if you have earned several. Some occupations involve a progression or series of certifications, and it is usually best to list all instead of just the highest level held.

Using inserts and enclosures has an advantage in addition to following the rule of brevity and clarity. It is also possible to tailor your résumé to the situation by including only those inserts or enclosures that apply to the company that you are interested in. The equipment list may not be appropriate for all positions, nor, perhaps, the list of professional associations. Therefore, these inserts may be omitted without affecting the continuity of the résumé.

Presenting the Résumé Packet

We are using the term *résumé packet* because in the following chapter, we will be discussing the importance of the cover letter, particularly for those in your situation. Therefore, the résumé packet will always contain at least two documents: the cover letter and the basic résumé. It may also contain a salary history, references, and any number of inserts and enclosures. We strongly recommend that the packet either be mailed or presented in a 9-by-12 envelope. It is always best to send it or deliver it to a specific person. If the person is not known, the department is the next best thing. Keep in mind, however, the point discussed in a previous chapter: if you have been given instructions either by an ad or person, follow them.

Sample Insert

The following shows the titling and the layout of a typical insert. The same format can be used for engineering projects, equipment lists, and so on.

ENGINEERING AND DESIGN PROJECTS

Stationary   Compressor Bleed Valve T/S
Multiple Purpose T/S
Hot Oil Bearing T/S
Proportioning Control T/S
A/C Generator/Alternator T/S
Hot Water Heater (Marine Corp)
Jet Engine Starter T/S
Compressor Overhaul T/S
Hydraulic Test Equipment for Canadian Airlines and Ford
   Motor Co.
Fuel Pumps and Fuel Control T/S for Curtiss Wright
Composite T/S to test Westinghouse Jet Engine
   Components
Fuel Component T/S for General Electric
Ethylene Glycol Stat. T/S
Special Filtering Network
Multipurpose Bench for Republic Valve
Single Engine Injector T/S
Turbine Driven Fuel Pump T/S, Thompson Products
Torpedo Components T/S, Newport, Rhode Island
Automotive Transmissions T/S
Afterburner Fuel Pump T/S
Hydrostatic Transmission T/S
Air Start–Jet Engine–Ready Squadrons

Portable   Lubricating Unit, Truck Mounted
Liquid O2 Purge Unit
MJ-1 Portable Hydraulic T/S (Detroit Diesel)
MJ-1 (Packette Engine)
MJ-2 (Packette Engine)
MK-3 Hydraulic Servicing Unit (Electric Motor)
Hydraulic Test Units for Commercial Airlines, Foreign
   and Domestic.

Letters That Get The Job

As you develop your résumé and begin to get involved in your job search, you will find that you will need several different types of letters in order to organize an effective search program. These letters are particularly appropriate for those of you changing careers or reentering. You can use three of the four to direct your background to your new career field.

The Letter of Application While some authors view the letter of application as a letter to accompany the résumé, the use of this term will be limited here to letters that are sent instead of the résumé. Background and experience are not easily adapted to the résumé format, particularly in the case of the reentering housewife. In this situation, there has been little or no direct work experience, although there may have been considerable activity that translates well to new career direction. If you fit this pattern, you should consider the use of the narrative letter to outline your interest in a position, the fact that you are reentering the work force, and why you think that you would be of value to the prospective employer. The letter should be brief; it can be particularly effective if you establish contact through a mutual acquaintance, a referral, or some other networking source. The letter of application is not very effective in shotgunning, that is, indiscriminately sending the letter to everyone in the industry. Nor is it recommended for larger companies because of their method of screening correspondence and applications. The exception in the large company would be the contact, someone that could help you get into the application stream. The letter of application is most effective in the smaller company or organization where the chances are greater that it will be read by someone who counts.

The Cover Letter (Letter of Transmittal)

The letter that accompanies the résumé in any of the four job search methods is called the cover letter or the letter of transmittal. In career change and reentry situations, it is an indispensable part of the résumé packet because it serves several very important functions.

First, the cover letter eliminates any surprises and should help establish a more receptive attitude on the part of the reader. It should clearly state the purpose and direction of your career move. In some cases, it should state the reason. For example, if you are changing careers because of conditions in your former occupation—plant closings or cutbacks, relocation, technical obsolescense—then these reasons can be stated. However, if the reasons are personal—divorce, death of a spouse, life-style change—they should not be mentioned in either the letter or the interview. In a reentry situation, it is acceptable to mention that your family is growing up and you want to return to active employment. It is not acceptable to go into the details of a divorce or other personal financial problems. The fact that you must work is of little importance to a prospective employer—the fact that you want to work can be of great importance.

Second, the cover letter should briefly summarize those parts of your background and experience that relate to your new career goal. This should occur in the second paragraph. At this point, you may also refer to any experience not mentioned in your résumé that may relate to the available position. In the second paragraph, indicate how your experience and your attitude can be of value to the employer. If appropriate, stress your previous work history.

Third, you can address the salary problem if a salary history is requested. Refer to the fact that you are aware that your salary history is not relevant because of your career change and point out that it is a negotiable item.

Fourth, use the cover letter to request a meeting or an interview to discuss how you can contribute to the employer's organization.

The cover letter also is used to establish contacts, referrals, recommendations, or mutual acquaintances. For example, "John Jones suggested that I write to you concerning the position of _____"; "I have been referred to you by the executive director of the association concerning the position of _____."

As with the résumé, the rule for cover letters is also brevity and clarity. Remember that this letter will also go through the various steps of the screening process along with the résumé and should enhance rather than detract from its effectiveness.

When you are applying for a specific position using a résumé with a general objective, use the cover letter to identify that position.

Sample Cover Letter for a Career Change

The following is an example of a cover letter that draws the reader's attention to the fact that you are seeking a career change. By using the cover letter in this manner, you eliminate any surprises or confusion as to why you are applying for the position after working in another career area. Your résumé should, in its objective and summary of qualifications, reinforce your new direction by further describing your experiences that can be translated to the industry you want to work in.

1234 East Road
Midtown, Ohio 12345
May 7, 1990

The Peirson Resort
Personnel Department
715 South Street
Watson, Texas 12345

Attn: Ms. Barbara Smith

Dear Ms. Smith:

Enclosed please find my résumé as application for the position of assistant food and beverage manager as advertised in the May 5, 1989 edition of the Watson Times.

Although this application represents a change in my career direction, my background and experience in management and customer relations should prove to be of value in the hospitality industry. Please note also that I was employed in the food and beverage industry on a part-time basis during the four years that I attended college.

I am enthusiastic about a career with the Peirson Chain and would appreciate the opportunity to meet with you, at your convenience, to discuss the possibility of my joining your staff.

Sincerely yours,

John H. James

The Follow-Up Letter

As the name implies, this letter is used to follow the submission of a résumé when you receive no initial response. The use of the follow-up letter is becoming somewhat obsolete as the number of résumés received by prospective employers continues to increase. Many companies have adopted the policy of not acknowledging the receipt of a résumé unless some further action or interest is contemplated.

Sample Cover Letter for a Specific Position

The following is an example of a letter of transmittal or a cover letter used to accompany a résumé directed at a specific position. Note that the date and placement of the ad is mentioned to identify the position.

125 Pine Street
Tacoma, Washington 12345
May 5, 1990

J. Wise & Co.
7215 Melba Street
Jackson, Wyoming 12345

Attn: Ms. Betty Jones

Dear Ms. Jones:

   Enclosed please find my résumé as application for the position of sales manager as advertised in the March 4, 1990, edition of the Wall Street Journal.
   I read with particular interest about your planned expansion into overseas markets. You will note that I have opened two overseas operations, one in Thailand and the other in Costa Rica. Both involved the development of a marketing plan and a sales force from scratch. In Costa Rica, I also assisted in the planning and construction of the first factory. In both instances, the operations were turning a profit within a year.
   I would appreciate the opportunity to meet with you to discuss how I may contribute to your organization.
   Thank you for your consideration.

Sincerely yours,

John Q. Doe

The Thank-You Letter   The thank-you letter is simply a matter of courtesy expressing your appreciation for the opportunity to meet with the prospective employer. Although one might think that this gesture would be automatic, hundreds of interviews with prospective employees often yield fewer than ten thank-you letters. The rest of those hundreds of applicants miss an opportunity to reintroduce themselves in a manner that is most positive. The letter itself should be brief, should mention the time and date of the interview and the position sought, and reemphasize your interest in both the organization and the position. It should be sent as soon after the interview as possible.

Sample Thank-You Letter

The following is a sample of a thank-you letter expressing appreciation for an interview and reaffirming interest in the position.

John A. James
12 South Street
Midtown, Ohio 12345
(111) 555-2233

Mr. Arnold Black, Vice President
Arnold Products, Inc.
1234 East Street
Midtown, Ohio 12345

Dear Mr. Black:

I would like to thank you for meeting with me at 9 a.m., June 5th, concerning the position of assistant manager in your customer support department and assure you of my continued interest.

I feel that it would be a challenging and rewarding career path and would consider it a privilege to be part of your team.

Again, my thanks for your time and consideration.

Sincerely yours,

John A. James

Worksheet: Letters That Get The Job

Practice writing your own letter on the following lines.

_____

_____

_____

_____

_____

_____

_____:

_____

_____

_____

_____

_____

_____

_____

_____

_____

_____

_____

_____

The Final Test: The Interview

10

Everything that has been discussed in the previous chapters has been leading up to this point: the interview. You should realize that being scheduled for an interview means that you have jumped some very important hurdles, particularly in situations involving a large number of applicants. You have not only met the requirements of the position, you have also probably been selected over numerous others who have also met the requirements. Before you even walk into the interview room, you have something going for you.

For those of you who have had little experience with the interview process, some time should be spent discussing the mechanics of interviewing, that is, the purpose of the interview and the various types of interviews. Later the preparations stage will be covered.

The Purpose of the Interview

Although some have termed the interview as a mutual exploratory process, in your situation there is apt to be less mutuality than most meetings between the prospective employer and employee. This is because you will be presenting more of a challenge to the interviewer, and thus the questioning and the discussion will probably be more penetrating and extensive. After all, you are not presenting a neat little employment package with all the background and experience falling into place. You are, however, presenting an interesting alternative to the normal career progression, or you would not be there.

Some interviews may involve some type of verbal or written test to further determine qualifications. However, most interviews involve only conversation, questions, and answers. Since your qualifications, experience, and education have already been noted and perhaps verified, the primary objective of the interviewer is to "size you up." The interviewer is interested in obtaining an impression of your character, stability, maturity, and your ability to fit into the organization and the work group. Talking about your experiences is an easy way to make you feel at ease or to guide the conversation into areas that the interviewer wishes to explore further. The extent of the interview and the number of interviewers will depend upon the type of interview or the stage of the interviewing process.

Types of Interviews

We must go back to the size and the type of the hiring organization to identify the various kinds of interviews that you may encounter. Those with very rigid hiring practices will have a structured interview format. Organizations whose hiring practices are informal may vary according to the pressures to fill the position and who is available to do the interviewing. Each interviewer has her or his own technique, and each organization will have differences in its interviewing procedures. The only way you can find out what your interviewing organization does is to ask. However, we can outline generally three interview classifications and the variations within each classification.

The preliminary or screening interview

In chapter 7 we described the process of elimination employers use to reduce the number of applicants from, for example, four hundred to the ten finalists. Some organizations will use the preliminary interview technique in the final stages of the reduction process to reduce the number from fifteen to ten or from ten to five. Those remaining after the cut then go on to the next stage of the selection process.

The preliminary interview is apt to be short—from five minutes to an hour—and usually the interviewer is from the personnel department or is a staff person from the department with the vacancy. Qualifications are usually reviewed and often the job and the organization are described in detail. This is done to establish the fact you are still interested in the position. The interviewer will often dominate the conversation in a preliminary interview. At this point, it is acceptable to ask for information concerning the overall selection process.

The preliminary interview is often used in smaller companies as the qualitative screening, depending on the number of applicants. Remember the résumé screening point that ensures that minimum requirements are met. If the number of applicants meeting minimum requirements is small, then it is a possibility that all of those remaining will obtain a preliminary interview.

Occasionally in academic or governmental circles even the preliminary interview will be conducted by a panel or a group of people from various sections of the organization. Here, advance information about hiring techniques can be very valuable, because to be forewarned is to be forearmed. Walking into an interview room and unexpectedly facing five interviewers instead of one can be very disconcerting.

The importance of the preliminary interview is obvious. It is another cut that you will have to survive, and your preparations have to be as detailed as for any other type of interview. It is very important that you again be honest about the fact that you are changing career directions or reentering. Usually the interviewer will not be the same person who has screened your résumé, so you will have to again translate your previous experience and education to the requirements of new career direction. Since the preliminary interviewer may not be very knowledgeable about the details of the position sought, her or his impression of you as being confident in your ability to do the job is very important.

The secondary interview (optional)

There are both quantitative and qualitative reviews. A quantitative review refers to a screening to determine the numbers involved in your background—number of years of work experience, supervisory experience, and education.

The quantitative review is concerned with the tangibles of your background.

The qualitative review refers to discovering the depth and the quality of your background—the levels of responsibilities and the amount of skill involved—in short, the extent of your background over and above the minimum requirements.

This two-step process is used in both résumé screening and interviewing. In the interviews, however, the qualitative review will be directed more toward your personality and character and your ability to get along with co-workers, subordinates, and superiors.

Most organizations will use a two-interview process: the preliminary and the final interview. However, a significant number of organizations interject a secondary interview, and the number is increasing. The secondary interview is always a qualitative review, since your minimum qualifications have long since been established. It will usually involve several people. You may meet these people one at a time or as a group. Regardless of the sequence, they will represent the various parts of the organization that you will be in contact with. Their primary purpose is to assess how you will fit in with the organization. Here we are back to the importance of first impressions. Although they may ask questions about your background, the odds are that they have all seen your résumé and the questions are asked more to see how you handle the response rather than what you say.

Usually the secondary interview is not an elimination or a cut interview. The finalists have already been selected. The secondary interview is used to provide the hiring authority with an extra dimension of opinion and to involve other departments as a matter of company relations and politics. Each of the people that you meet will forward her or his opinions to the hiring authority. The extent to which these opinions will influence the selection varies from not at all to completely. Obviously you have to play the game according to the latter possibility.

The final interview   Sometimes known as "going for all the marbles," the final interview is the culmination of all your efforts to obtain the position. But what do you know before you enter the room? First you know that the emphasis will be on the intangibles—your confidence, your ability to relate, your interest in the organization, and your general attitude—rather than specific details about your background. Be pre-

pared to answer questions about your choice of a new career direction.

Second, if you have already had a secondary interview
involving several people, then the odds are that the final
will be with one person. That will probably be the person
with either the power to make the final choice or the power
to veto the selection if it has been made by others.

Third, if there has not been a secondary interview, then
be prepared to meet with several people, either one at a
time or in a group. Usually you will be told during the
screening interview whether you will be interviewed by a
formal search committee or if you will meet others in your
work group.

When faced with multiple interviews, your first question may be, "Who has the final say?" Who is most influential in making the final decision? These are difficult questions to answer because each organization has its own
patterns and procedures. However, there are several facts
that you should be aware of when trying to answer these
questions.

- If there is a formal search committee involved, then
  you are dealing with an organization that probably is
  subject to strict affirmative action and equal opportunity guidelines. The search committee will either
  make the choice or make the recommendation to the
  hiring authority. The recommendation, in reality, is
  seldom vetoed or changed.

- If you meet informally with a number of people related to your potential job, these people's opinions are
  in no way binding upon the hiring authority.

- In the larger organization, someone from the personnel department will be involved in the whole procedure. How influential this person will be depends
  upon the status of the personnel department. If it is
  extremely "turf conscious," very protective about its
  authority, then personnel will be in on the whole process to the very end. In some cases, personnel will
  hold the veto power. As one director of personnel
  stated, "The decision as to who is to be hired is made
  jointly by myself and the division head." Within a
  very short time after beginning the interview process, you will be able to sense who is in charge, the

personnel department or the hiring department.

- In situations not involving a formal search committee, it is a safe bet that the most influential person will be the immediate supervisor or the section manager. There are few managers or directors who force their decisions upon those who have to supervise the employees. For example, if you are interviewing for a position in a local agency headed by a manager and the hiring authority is the regional manager, the local manager's selection will be followed, even though the actual appointment is made at the regional level.

How to Prepare for the Interview Process

Preparing for the interview is like preparing for a final examination—first you must learn the information and then you must psych yourself up to take the exam. The first part of this section will concentrate on the information part of the process, and the second section will cover the emotional preparation necessary.

Your situation demands that you must selectively direct portions of your education and background toward the requirements of a desired position or career. That was the purpose of the résumé worksheet—to identify those portions or segments that could be used. As you apply for specific positions, you will need to further refine your list in order to concentrate on that target. However, you cannot do this effectively until you know as much as possible about your target. It is essential that you learn about the position and the organization in order to organize your thoughts and your approach to possible problem areas in which you feel that you may be short in qualifications.

Sources of information

Your first task is to obtain a complete job description and an organizational chart of the department in which the vacancy exists. The organizational chart is a chart showing the relationships of the various positions within the department. It will show you the subordinate, the equal, and the superior positions. That knowledge will be of considerable help if the interview involves several people or a search committee.

Often you will be given a complete job description when you are notified of your selection to be interviewed. If not, do not be afraid to ask. Asking can do nothing but reinforce, in their eyes, your interest in the position. In fact, be as visible as possible. Obtaining the organizational chart could be considerably more difficult. Some organizations do not have them, or if they do, the charts are not considered to be for public distribution. Your inquiry can be directed to the personnel department or to the department filling the vacancy. If a chart is not available, ask for a description of the department: number of employees, who reports to whom (by position title), and how the department relates to the rest of the organization.

Information about the organization in general can be obtained from a variety of sources: chamber of commerce, Better Business Bureau, the public relations department of the company itself, or current or past employees. If the organization is a corporation, try to obtain a copy of the annual report. You are looking for positive aspects of working for the organization. You will find a dozen opportunities to use this information during the course of the interviews. If you find considerable negative information, then perhaps you should let this position go by.

Organizing your presentation and response patterns

Although employers are becoming increasingly familiar with career changers and reentries, the odds are that most of your competition—the other candidates—will be following a normal career pattern. Consequently, you will undoubtedly be asked questions about why you left your former career and why you chose this career. Develop a logical response to these questions without referring to personal situations. Memorize it or at least become sufficiently familiar with the response so that you can paraphrase it accurately. Do the same for your education and experience that relates to the position. Try to cover every function in the job description and tie in portions of your background to those functions.

Maintaining your balance

There are several tendencies that reduce some job applicants' effectiveness during the interview process. First, they display a certain air of superiority and haughtiness. Perhaps their attitude is designed to portray confidence; if so, that is not the impression that is given the interviewer. Second, those who are older than other candidates and could use their maturity as an advantage often don't.

Third, many talk endlessly and compulsively about why they are making a change. This is often true of those who are involved in a divorce or the death of a spouse. But the employer does not want to hear about how unfairly your former spouse treated you or how your husband left you without a cent or how your exwife cleaned you out. One client, a man in his early fifties, had gone through a messy divorce. He obtained numerous interviews but never got beyond first base. He was relating every detail of the divorce to the prospective employers. Finally he was convinced to keep his mouth shut about his problems, and he got the next job.

It is perfectly normal to be nervous about an interview; sometimes even the interviewer is nervous. In some people, nervousness will result in a compulsion to talk, in some cases even disregarding the interviewer's question. When we use the term *balance*, we refer to confidence without being superior, listening instead of talking, and an aura of being in control.

Use your maturity to your advantage. Although much of your experience may not be applicable to the position you are interviewing for, much of it relates to the situation. That is to say, you have met stressful circumstances before and therefore know what to expect.

The same thing can be said for those reentering the job market. There is no reason to consider yourself inferior. You have as much life experience as the interviewer, probably more. Maintaining the proper balance is a matter of placing everything in the proper perspective and realizing your own worth as a person.

Dressing for the part

In an earlier part of this book, we discussed how our clothing may add to our self-esteem. Certainly you will want to feel good about yourself in this respect when you present yourself for an interview. Clothing may not make the man or woman, but it does add to the impression you make on others. There are many books written about dressing for successful careers. If you are in doubt or plan to invest any amount of money in a new wardrobe, you may want to browse through some of these. What we will offer here are only some commonsense suggestions with which you can start.

What you wear to an interview will, and should, add to the window dressing of total self. Begin by using the information you have gathered about the prospective company you are interviewing for. Who will you be interviewing for? Where will the interview take place? Sometimes there are practicalities that must be taken into consideration. For instance, you would probably not want to wear extremely high heels if you were expected to walk through a construction site or a three-piece suit to a horse ranch.

Common sense will get you a long way. Clean and neat are an absolute: no buttons missing goes without saying. To be fashionable does not mean trendy. Stick to basics to be safe. Believe it or not, some establishments remain extremely conservative. Some even have dress codes. The suit with a white shirt and conservative tie is always safe. A blazer or solid-colored sportcoat and slacks is a bit more casual but may be even more appropriate under some circumstances.

Women have more choices of color and style and also have more opportunity to err. Slacks may be worn by the women at the job site, but they are not a good choice for an interview. Dresses are very acceptable if they are conservative and tailored. They should have neither low neck lines nor high hem lines. Colors should be flattering; a solid color is considered more businesslike than a pattern.

Suits, blazers, and skirts give one a finished appearance and are probably the best choice. These can be expensive, though, and if you are not able to make this sort of initial investment, a skirt and blouse can certainly qualify. We are speaking of a skirt without slits, well fitting, and a blouse that is tailored, fresh looking, and not sheer. Jewelry is an accessory and not to be overdone.

For either men or women, neat hair; polished shoes in good condition; and clean, well-shaped nails are essential. Don't overdo the cologne, whether it is aftershave or perfume; stick with the lighter scents. If you are careful and organized with the details of your dress, it will show. It adds to your packaging which in turn enhances the first impression you will have on others. As a last word of advice, make your decisions about your clothing ahead of time; don't wait until the last minute to throw things together. It will be less nerve-wracking when you get the call to come in for an interview. You will also have had the time to try out different touches to see which works the best for you.

Worksheet: Checklist to Prepare For an Interview

I'm interviewing for the position of: _____

The company is: _____

address: _____

_____

phone: _____

My appointment is set for: _____

The person confirming the appointment was: _____

I'll be interviewing with: (name) _____

(title) _____

Any specific instructions I've been given or directions I need: _____

_____

_____

For this job my strongest points are: _____

_____

_____

_____

_____

_____

Questions I have are: _____

_____

_____

_____

Preparing Emotionally and Mentally

You are now an old hand at getting yourself ready for the next step. The interview is no different. It is merely another step, another stage to get through. It is a part of the whole process. You've come this far with your plan, and you will indeed complete this step too. All your work and effort will pay off.

Let's go through the accomplishments you have already made. First, there was the need to deal with any negative feelings. By now those have been safely defused, right? Next you went on to learn a lot more about yourself; you reached an understanding and acceptance of who and what you are. You have dealt with the realities of your situation and the job prospect. You set goals and made a decision that has brought you to this point. Your self-confidence has grown. Being given the opportunity for this interview is a crowning touch.

You've made many preparations all along the way. Don't stop now. When you know the date and time of your interview, start the preparations for it immediately. Leave nothing to chance. Make sure your car will start. Be sure the gas gauge will not be on empty. Get your clothes ready. If you need a babysitter, arrange for it and for a backup just in case. We've all heard of Murphy's Law: "Anything that can go wrong, will." Be especially careful that it does not by planning ahead for any event that might throw you off your schedule or make you anxious.

One short reminder about your self-confidence: you will cut your anxiety level in half if you feel good about yourself, pleased with the way you look, and comfortable with your preparations. The less anxious you are, the more confident you will feel and appear. Nervous? That's normal, but you can use that to your advantage. It will give you the edge that you need to listen better and to perform with prudence.

Once at the interview, take a couple of deep breaths and try to relax. As you get out of your car, leave all the rest of your concerns and problems suspended on the car's ceiling. Lock them in there—they'll be safe until you return. From that moment on, use your energy to concentrate on each and every moment as it occurs. Fine tune your mind and observations and be conscious of every move you make. That kind of concentration will block your nervousness. If you must wait for someone, then use the time to run through your self-marketing process. Organize your strong points once again so you will be ready to sell them.

During the interview itself, be employer oriented. Note your interviewer's style. Is it formal, informal, too casual? Do not fall into the trap of being casual in return. You need not appear stiff, but it is more appropriate and professional to remain on the formal side. Answer questions as directly and concisely as you can. Do not fear a pause to contemplate on one of your answers. Again, keep your personal problems out of the interview. The interview process is an impersonal one; keep that in mind. If you should be asked about personal aspects of your life, answer them as briefly as possible. Listen carefully and effectively; when it is appropriate, ask the questions you have thought out (and phrased) in advance. Use good body language throughout the entire interview. Be attentive, sit up straight, and maintain good eye contact.

Once the interview has concluded, thank the person or persons who have just interviewed you. You may want to know when they expect to make a decision if that has not already been discussed. As you leave, be sure to stop and thank anyone else who has been of help to you, such as a secretary or a receptionist. That very same day or evening, write a thank-you letter to the interviewer which again expresses your gratitude for receiving the interview. When you must interview more than once for the same job or for numerous jobs, learn from the previous ones: practice makes better.

Operating Your Own Business 11

Probably some of you, as you made the decision to change careers or to come back into the work force, thought about having your own business. Some dismissed the idea immediately—too risky, no start-up capital, no strong inclination toward any particular type of business. Others of you still have the idea tucked away in the back of your mind that one of these days you might start out on your own. Look around you at the new businesses in your community. Almost every one has been started by someone who used to work for someone else, often in a completely different field or endeavor. So operating your own business is an alternative.

Despite all the attention given to the corporate giants, small business still represents over 90 percent of all businesses in the United States today. Small business employs over 50 percent of the nation's labor force and produces over 50 percent of all business receipts. In fact, most of the growth in employment during the eighties took place in the small business sector.

However, operating your own business is not without its risks. It is estimated that 50 percent of new businesses fail within the first five years. No one really knows how accurate this percentage is, because the only statistics available are those failures involving bankruptcy. Thousands of other businesses quietly take their losses and close the doors. There are ways, however, to substantially reduce the risk of failure in business start-ups or acquisitions, which we will discuss in this chapter.

It is beyond the scope of this book to become involved in a detailed discussion of how to start up or acquire a business. But it is such an important alternative that we will provide some suggestions about how to investigate your business opportunities and what you must consider before you decide to go into business.

Several years ago, numerous entrepreneurs were interviewed, some very successful, some not so successful, and some who had failed. Without exception, they all stressed the importance of a good advisory team, especially those who had failed. They also stressed the need for adequate operating capital, since many types of businesses do not operate in the black for two to five years. They also noted that the determination of how much working capital would be adequate was one of the functions of the advisory team. Therefore, if you are thinking of starting or acquiring a business, put together a group of people that can advise you in all of the critical areas of business operations before you make any moves.

Your Advisory Team

The core of your team should consist of three people: an accountant, a lawyer, and a financial advisor. All three should have expertise in small business operations. The lawyer should be knowledgeable about taxes and business structures; the accountant should be familiar with the reporting requirements of various types of business; the financial advisor should have expertise in various types of financing and working capital requirements. You should also have a source of information for market analysis and labor laws.

Your accountant should be able to design a system that does more than just provide a record of transactions for tax purposes. An accounting system's primary function is to provide information for use in managing the business, that is, timely information about expenses, income, cash flow, and ratios important to the analysis of business operations.

Your advisory team can be hired on a fee basis, they can be members of your board of directors, or they can be members of an informal or quasi-board of advisors. Regardless of the structure, remember that having these advisors is the foremost advice of people who have been there—experienced entrepreneurs.

Start, Buy, or Franchise? Starting from scratch

Have you ever known people who felt they had such a terrific idea for starting a business that the banks just had to lend them the money? They didn't get very far, did they? Banks are more aware of the percentages of new businesses that fail than anyone else. They are very wary of lending money for start-up unless it can be backed up by a mortgage on your house or guaranteed by someone else, such as the Small Business Administration (SBA). It is very difficult to finance a new business starting from scratch. Most new businesses are privately financed with owner's money and loans from friends and relatives, a fact that also explains why so many are undercapitalized. The magazines, however, are filled with stories about people who started businesses requiring a minimum of capital. They started very small, working out of their homes, not overcommitting themselves. In many cases, they had other sources of income so that they did not have to pull money out of the business until it had matured. It took time, time that you may not have.

You have two other alternatives to starting a business from scratch. You can buy an existing business or you can buy into a franchise. In both cases, your risk is significantly less, and, consequently, financing may be a little easier to obtain.

Buying a business

Banks and other investors will view the purchase of an existing business in a more positive light because that business has a track record, a history that is valuable in determining the risk involved. If the business is successful and established, their attention will be directed to you—they will want to know if you are qualified to take over the business and continue to make a profit.

Use your team whenever you consider buying an existing business. Have the accountant review prior financial records and current assets; have your lawyer review all existing leases, contracts, patterns, and other commitments; have your financial advisor review the terms of the sale, the appraisal of assets, and any debt instruments involved.

Also examine the reason the owner is selling. If the business has been profitable, is there anything that threatens to change that—a new highway affecting traffic patterns, a plant closing, a zoning change, or new competition opening up across the street?

Franchising

Your other option is to buy into a franchise. A franchise is a form of licensing involving a product, service, or method. The franchisor licenses you, the franchisee, to market the product or service according to the terms required by the franchise agreement. Operating a reputable and successful franchise reduces your risk considerably. According to the National Franchise Association, fewer than 5 percent of franchises fail, a percentage far lower than the estimates for new businesses in general. The advantage of dealing with less risk will cost you in the form of franchise fees, royalties or a percentage of the gross, and a loss of flexibility and freedom in operating your business. For those of you who have never been in business before, the cost may be well worth the reduced risk. Financing is usually easier to obtain in a franchise situation because the franchise usually has an established history with an identifiable market, and the lenders or investors have a greater assurance of success.

If you are interested in franchising, obtain a copy of the *Franchise Opportunities Handbook* published by the United States Department of Commerce and sold through the Office of the Superintendent of Documents, U.S. Government Printing Office, Washington, DC 20402. This publication will provide considerable information about franchising in general and lists most of the franchises presently registered in the United States. It also provides much information about these franchises, including the number of franchises, the product or service, the cost, and the training offered by the franchisor.

We offer a word of caution. The franchising concept has spread through many industries over the past two decades. As with any successful idea, franchising has attracted its share of the unscrupulous and the dishonest. Bring in your advisory team when investigating any franchise. You will also find that the reputable franchisors will investigate you as much as you investigate them. The reputation of the franchise and the recognition of its logo or trademark is critical to the ultimate success of the franchise. Consequently, the franchisors try to keep as many bad apples as possible out of the barrel.

One of the most important items of information needed when evaluating a franchise is the disclosure statement, sometimes called the offering circular or prospectus. Nationwide use of the disclosure statement is required by the Federal Trade Commission and by many state regulations. Any franchise that indicates that it does not have a prospectus or a disclosure statement should be crossed off your list immediately.

The disclosure statement should include information concerning twenty to twenty-five subjects involving the franchise, including some of these critical questions:

- Who are the franchisor and their affiliates, and what is their business experience?

- What is the business experience of the officers and the principles?

- Have they been involved in any previous lawsuits or bankruptcies?

- Are all fees, commission or royalty schedules, downpayments, and other financial requirements fully disclosed?

- What are the restrictions, limitations, and requirements involved in the production of the goods or services? Are there restricted specifications involved— are you required to purchase only from the franchisor?

- Are you guaranteed exclusive territories or locations?

- Under what conditions can the franchise be repurchased, sold, transferred, or terminated?

- Is there any financing available through the franchisor?

- What training, advertising, and promotional assistance is provided?

- Are financial statements available, and are they audited?

- Is there statistical information available about the current franchisee?

These are just a few of the questions that the disclosure statement should answer. A more complete list can be found in the *Franchise Opportunities Handbook.*

Do not assume that all of the information in the statement is accurate. Do some checking with existing franchisees in your marketing area. Most will be quite frank as long as you are not a potential competitor. Check also any claims about sales, income, or profits provided by the franchisor. Part of the regulations by the Federal Trade Commission require that if claims are made about potential earnings, volume, or profits, they must be substantiated. Be certain you also understand on what assumptions the earnings estimates or reports are based—labor costs, interest rate levels, amounts of financing, volume levels. Check with several franchisees about their first-year earnings so that you can estimate your working capital requirements with greater accuracy.

As a prospective franchisee, you have certain legal rights under federal law. Your attorney should be able to advise you what these rights are.

The *Franchise Opportunities Handbook* also has an excellent checklist for use in the investigation and the evaluation of franchises.

Choosing the Proper Business Structure

Every beginning business must choose what form or structure to assume when it first opens its doors. About 65 to 70 percent of the businesses in United States today gross under $500,000 per year, and the majority of these are classified as sole proprietorships or DBA's (doing business as). As a business grows, it is normal for the owners to change their structure several times, and their needs as well as the needs of the business also change. Your choices of business structures include the following:

- sole proprietorship or DBA
- partnership
- closely held or family corporation
- public corporation
- S corporations (formerly subchapter S corporations)

In making a choice as important as a business structure, your advisory team should come into play, especially since the choice will involve consideration of many factors. The team will first determine what structure will be most suited to your current tax situation. It will then consider such factors as exposure to liability, the amount of assets pledged for initial financing, who controls the business, whether the business will continue if the principal dies or is incapacitated, and whether other members of the family will be involved. It is also possible that the team will advise organizing as one type in the beginning and then reorganizing as another once the business grows.

Again, obtain professional advisors. Your selection must be done carefully and with considerable investigation. Unfortunately, both the legal and the tax fields have their share of daredevils, people who enjoy brinkmanship and the manipulation of laws and regulations. If these people were employed by a circus, they would be the ones on the high wires and in the lion's cage. They are in the legal and tax fields, however, because they can still play daredevil, but with other people's lives and money. The field of law and taxation is a field of opinions and interpretation with more shades of gray than a basket of dirty laundry. Your advice must come from a team of intelligent professionals with a track record of sensing the direction and the current spirit of the law, a team that doesn't continually require that you be the one to gamble to enhance their reputation.

Also, be emotionally and mentally prepared, particularly if you have been forced into making a move. Operating your own business can require tremendous amounts of energy, concentration, and stamina. Being successful, however, can be immensely rewarding. One of the keys to success is being emotionally ready to meet the challenges.

The following checklist concerning your present status and your goals is to be used as a guide in determining the best business format for your particular situation, but remember that your business and overall business conditions are in a constant state of change. This checklist, therefore, should be reviewed periodically.

Ownership

- Do you wish to own the business entirely?
- Do you plan to divide ownership with your spouse or children?
- Do you wish to keep control or a majority position even though ownership is distributed?
- Do you plan to bring investors into the business?

- Are you planning to acquire an existing business?

- Do you plan on eventually going public?

- Will you have loans on which you have pledged personal assets?

- Do you want the business or the proceeds from the business to go to members of your family in the event of your death?

- Do you have several children, not all of whom are interested in continuing the business?

- Do you anticipate sale of the business before your retirement?

Financial

- Do you have any sources of income other than the business?

- Does your spouse's employment provide medical and insurance benefits?

- Are you able to shelter income to the maximum allowed by HR 10s, and IRAs?

- Do you anticipate the need for substantial financing in the future?

- Do you have substantial personal assets that can be pledged for business loans?

- Would corporate status offer you substantial tax breaks for business expenses?

- Do you have access to private investment capital?

- Do you plan to do business in more than one state?

- Do you plan to limit the number of investors?

- Do you plan to try to raise venture capital?

Miscellaneous

- Are you concerned about the details of your business being made public?

- Are you or your investors looking for tax losses to shelter other income?

- Would you want to give up total or partial control of your business to a board of directors?

Review your answers to the above questions to determine which structure best suits your needs at this time. You will also want to discuss all problems with your advisors before you begin and on a continuing basis as well as researching all areas on your own.

Appendix: Recommended Reading

Bolles, Richard. *What Color Is Your Parachute?* Ten Speed Press, annually updated.

Catalyst Staff. *Marketing Yourself.* New York: Bantam Books, 1981

Curtis, Jean. *Working Mothers.* Garden City, N.Y.: Double Day & Co., 1976

Donnaha, Melvin, and John L. Meyer. *How to Get the Job You Want.* Prentice Hall, N.J.: Spectrum Books, 1976

Ellis, Albert, and Robert Harper. *A Guide to Rational Living.* North Hollywood, Calif.: Wilshire Book Company, 1974 ed.

Fensterheim, Herbert and Jean Baer. *Don't Say Yes When You Want to Say No.* New York: Dell Publishing Company, 1975.

Fucini, Joseph J. and Susy Fucini. *Entrepreneurs: The Men and Women Behind Famous Brand Names and How They Made It.* Boston: G. K. Hall & Company, 1985

Jones, Rochelle. *The Big Switch: New Careers, New Lives after 35.* New York: McGraw-Hill, 1980.

Kerr, Clark, and Jerome M. Resow, eds. *Work in America: The Decade Ahead.* New York: Van Nostrand Reinhold Company, 1979.

Keyes, Ken, Jr. *Handbook to Higher Consciousness.* 4th ed. Berkeley: The Living Love Center, 1974.

Lair, Jess. *I Ain't Well But I Sure Am Better.* Garden City, N.Y.: Doubleday & Company, 1975.

Lathrop, Richard. *Who's Hiring Who.* Berkeley: Ten Speed Press, 1977.

Lott, Catherine S. and Oscar C. Lott. *How to Land a Better Job.* Lincolnwood, Ill.: VGM Career Horizons, 1989.

Newman, Mildred, and Bernard Berkowitz. *How to Be Your Own Best Friend.* New York: Random House, 1982

O'Neil, Nina, and George O'Neil. *Shifting Gears.* New York: Avon Books, 1975.

Paradis, Adrian. *Opportunities in Your Own Service Business.* Lincolnwood, Ill.: VGM Career Horizons, 1985.

Pogrebin, Letty Cottin. *Getting Yours.* New York: Avon Books, 1976.

Schwartz, Alvin. *The Unions: What They Are, How They Came to Be, How They Affect Us.* New York: Viking Press, 1972.

Sheehy, Gail. *Passages.* New York: Bantam Books, 1977.

Smith, Manual J. *When I Say No, I Feel Guilty.* New York: Bantam Books, 1975.

Viscott, David. *Risking.* New York: Pocket Books, 1977.

Wilkie, Jane. *The Divorced Woman's Handbook: An Outline for Starting the First Year Alone.* New York: William Morrow & Company, 1980.

Zaki, Elinor P. and Margaret M. Mangold. *Interviewing, Its Principle and Methods.* New York: Family Service Association of America, 1972.

VGM CAREER BOOKS

CAREER DIRECTORIES
Careers Encyclopedia
Dictionary of Occupational
    Titles
Occupational Outlook
    Handbook

CAREERS FOR
Animal Lovers
Bookworms
Computer Buffs
Crafty People
Culture Lovers
Environmental Types
Film Buffs
Foreign Language Aficionados
Good Samaritans
Gourmets
History Buffs
Kids at Heart
Nature Lovers
Night Owls
Number Crunchers
Plant Lovers
Shutterbugs
Sports Nuts
Travel Buffs

CAREERS IN
Accounting; Advertising;
Business; Child Care;
Communications; Computers;
Education; Engineering;
the Environment; Finance;
Government; Health Care;
High Tech; Journalism; Law;
Marketing; Medicine;
Science; Social &
Rehabilitation Services

CAREER PLANNING
Admissions Guide to Selective
    Business Schools
Beating Job Burnout
Beginning Entrepreneur
Career Planning &
    Development for College
    Students & Recent Graduates
Career Change

Careers Checklists
Cover Letters They Don't
    Forget
Executive Job Search Strategies
Guide to Basic Cover Letter
    Writing
Guide to Basic Resume Writing
Guide to Temporary
    Employment
Job Interviews Made Easy
Joyce Lain Kennedy's Career
    Book
Out of Uniform
Resumes Made Easy
Slam Dunk Resumes
Successful Interviewing for
    College Seniors
Time for a Change

CAREER PORTRAITS
Animals	Nursing
Cars	Sports
Computers	Teaching
Music	Travel

GREAT JOBS FOR
Communications Majors
English Majors
Foreign Language Majors
History Majors
Psychology Majors

HOW TO
Approach an Advertising
    Agency and Walk Away with
    the Job You Want
Bounce Back Quickly After
    Losing Your Job
Choose the Right Career
Find Your New Career Upon
    Retirement
Get & Keep Your First Job
Get Hired Today
Get into the Right Business
    School
Get into the Right Law School
Get People to Do Things Your
    Way
Have a Winning Job Interview

Hit the Ground Running in
    Your New Job
Improve Your Study Skills
Jump Start a Stalled Career
Land a Better Job
Launch Your Career in TV
    News
Make the Right Career Moves
Market Your College Degree
Move from College into a
    Secure Job
Negotiate the Raise You
    Deserve
Prepare a Curriculum Vitae
Prepare for College
Run Your Own Home Business
Succeed in College
Succeed in High School
Write a Winning Resume
Write Successful Cover Letters
Write Term Papers & Reports
Write Your College Application
    Essay

OPPORTUNITIES IN
This extensive series provides
detailed information on nearly
150 individual career fields.

RESUMES FOR
Advertising Careers
Banking and Financial Careers
Business Management Careers
College Students &
    Recent Graduates
Communications Careers
Education Careers
Engineering Careers
Environmental Careers
50 + Job Hunters
Health and Medical Careers
High School Graduates
High Tech Careers
Law Careers
Midcareer Job Changes
Sales and Marketing Careers
Scientific and Technical Careers
Social Service Careers
The First-Time Job Hunter

 VGM Career Horizons
a division of *NTC Publishing Group*
4255 West Touhy Avenue
Lincolnwood, Illinois 60646–1975